Trapped In Paradise
Views of My Cuba

Trapped In Paradise
Views of My Cuba

Richard M. Grove

Hidden Brook Press

Second Edition

Hidden Brook Press
www.HiddenBrookPress.com
writers@HiddenBrookPress.com

Copyright © 2011 Richard M. Grove

All rights for writing revert to the author. All rights for book, layout and design remain with Hidden Brook Press. No part of this book may be reproduced except by a reviewer who may quote brief passages in a review. The use of any part of this publication reproduced, transmitted in any form or by any means, electronic, mechanical, photocopied, recorded or otherwise stored in a retrieval system without prior written consent of the publisher is an infringement of the copyright law.

Trapped In Paradise: Views of My Cuba by Richard M. Grove

Layout and Design – Richard M. Grove
Photographs – Richard M. Grove
Cover Design – Richard M. Grove
Cover Digital Painting – Richard M. Grove

Printed and bound in Canada

Library and Archives Canada Cataloguing in Publication

Grove, Richard M. (Richard Marvin), 1953-
    Trapped in paradise : views of my Cuba / Richard M. Grove.

ISBN 978-1-897475-57-7

    1. Grove, Richard M. (Richard Marvin), 1953- --Travel--Cuba. 2. Cuba--Description and travel. 3. Cuba--Poetry. I. Title.

PS8563.R75T73 2010   C818'.5409   C2010-905483-0

Manuel

Dedicated to:

Mi Hermano / My Brother Manuel.

Thank you *mi amigo* for your family, love and support.

Also to my darling wife Kim, *mi esposa, mi amor, mi amiga,* my life traveller.

Eric

List of Poems

- Cemetery Walk – *p. 37*
- submerged echo – *p. 40*
- Outstretched Hands – *p. 47*
- What Day Is It? – *p. 48*
- Joshua's Version – *p. 48*
- Ox Cart Plod – *p. 50*
- Eternal Hope – *p. 52*
- Origami for the Beggar Lady – *p. 54*
- Enthusiasm – *p. 55*
- Overcoming Hills – *p. 57*
- Arriving in Santiago de Cuba – *p. 80*
- A White Chalk Line Marked Her Past – *p. 83*
- 2008 – Cuevas de Bellamar
  / – The Caves of Bellemar – *p. 112*

Table of Contents

– Preface – *p. 7*
– Foreword – *p. 39*
– Arriving – *p. 40*
– Rural Work Ethic – *p. 48*
– Moving to Holguín – *p. 52*
– December 09 / 09 – *p. 55*
– Santiago de Cuba Departure – *p. 56*
– The Sugarcane Juice Booth – *p. 57*
– A Long Day – *p. 60*
– The Ride in the Big Blue Truck Story – *p. 62*
– A Memorable Face – *p. 64*
– Arriving in Palma Soriano – *p. 65*
– The Sleeping in the Brothel Story – *p. 67*
– A 5 am Departure – *p. 72*
– The Coffee In the Ditch Story – *p. 76*
– Coffee on the Roof – *p. 82*
– Sunday Morning On The Front Porch of Roberto's Casa – *p. 84*
– Roberto – *p. 89*
– Another Episode of Generosity – *p. 91*
– Cuba and the Bent Wheel Parallel – *p. 93*
– A Trip to Gibara – *p. 100*
– A Visit to the Caves of Gibara – *p. 102*
– The Silence of Black – *p. 104*
– Laundry and the Dead Windmill – *p. 118*
– A Trip to a Distant Farm – *p. 119*
– Cultural Differences – *p. 122*
– Viva la Revolución – *p. 125*
– There was no Squeal of a Pig – *p. 127*
– Afterword – *p. 140*

– Biographical Sketch of Author – *p. 142*

Mother and daughter in the town of Gibara

*Thank you to Donna Langevin
for your copyedits and kind support
for this second edition.
I hope I implemented all of the changes.*

Preface

Cuba is one of my favourite travel destinations. My wife Kim and I have been to Germany, France, England, the USA, a short stopover in Mexico and three glorious weeks in New Zealand but after almost 30 visits, Cuba has become my second home. After I returned to Canada in February, 2010, from a month-long visit I gathered my notes and started to write this book, Trapped in Paradise. What a wonderful memory it has become. I had almost as much fun remembering and writing about the trip as I did on the actual trip.

    Being with my two friends, mis amigos, Eric and Manuel for the bicycle part of the trip was a lifetime highlight to say the least; brothers bonding in the heat of a Cuban day, Royal Palms lazily drifting by, strangers hooting or tooting to us with camaradic waves as we passed. Red-headed turkey vultures kited overhead, ash grey zebu with floppy humps, munching time, didn't bother to lift their black-horned heads as we swished past their grazing patch. Stoic salt-white egrets sporting striking ebony feet and beaks nodded to us from their back-perched, insect-pecking vantage point. The smell of hot pavement, salt-stained drips from brow dotted our path past emerald fields of sugarcane. Precious few clouds filtered amid the brilliant sun-squinting sky as we darted from one freckle-shaded spot to another. We pushed towards the saw-toothed mountain range of La Sierra Maestra far in the distance. Mile by mile, pedal push by pedal push, we drew closer to our ocean-side destination. We really did cross those mountains. Amazing! Absolutely amazing. By bicycle there is no going around them – 250 km long by 60 km wide. The tallest peak is 1,974 metres above sea level, the highest sky-scraping heights in all of Cuba but finally we glided into the friendly embrace of Santiago de Cuba's hustle and bustle.

  Originally I was going to bike on my own but quickly, without hesitation, my dear friend, my true brother, Manuel decided to join me. How could I refuse his camaraderie and the guidance that he would bring. Then before you know it my Toronto friend Eric – I call him Ereeco, invited himself along. I embraced his interest in sharing my adventure. Even though I had known Ereeco for decades it turned out to be a wonderful bonding time. So there we were three middle-aged city slickers, non-drinkers, spiritually oriented friends heading out together each with his own unrevealed expectations, hopes and dreams to be filled. It very much reminded me of the youthful spirit of my late teens and early twenties, hitchhiking across Canada – four or five times in total.

  Below is how the story unfolded. I so much hope you enjoy travelling with me through these pages.

Sincerely
Tai / Richard M. Grove

```
-----Original Message-----
From: "Richard Grove" <writers@hiddenbrookpress.com>
Sent: 04/10/2009 6:05 PM
To: "Manuel León" <manuel.vl@hlg.rimed.cu>
Subject: november 27th
```

my brother

we will be arriving in cuba on november 27th - Bill, Juli, Joshua, Kim and me. we will be staying at the same ocean side resort as we did with the ccla our last trip. flying in to holguin with bus to the resort in Guardalavaca - i will give you more details later.

everyone will be staying for one week. i will be staying for three extra weeks with my bicycle. i plan on bicycling to santiago - you can bike with me or you can meet me there or i can meet you later in Holguin — which ever is best for you my friend. i would love to have you with me but i know how busy you are. i do not wish to impose on your schedule.

i am going to take it very slow. i am going to write a book and meditate all the way there. my odd plan is that i am going to bike and stop every fifteen minutes and take pictures and write in my diary. i will stop for 3 minutes or 1 hour or longer if my mind and body tell me to. i am going to let my inner being guide me. this is my fantastic plan.

once i get to santiago i would like to find
a casa particular and stay for a few days
near or on the ocean. i am so burned out
right now that i need time to read,
meditate, swim, eat and sleep. - you can do
that with me if your heart and time permits
- but no one else. this will be a mindful
slow pace holiday not a party time. then i
plan on taking the bus back to holguin and
put my feet under your table and stay in a
casa there until i fly home.

i hope that you, pablo and adonay will be
able to come to the resort and spend the day
with us on the beach and we will take you
out to lunch and dinner there. maybe your
friend - Mariam - with the car can come
again. one thing that i hope is that this
visit will take place at the end of the one
week and that i will send some things with
you in the car to holguin - things that i
will not need on my bike.

this may sounds like a crazy plan but god
will be with me - with us - all the way. i
have dreamed of this for months

hugs to everyone

tai

-----Original Message-----
From: "Manuel León" <manuel.vl@hlg.rimed.cu>
Sent: 05/10/2009 3:13 PM
To:"RichardGrove@spamarrest.com"
<RichardGrove@spamarrest.com
Subject: Wonderful

My brother,

It's so wonderful, so great! We are already pushing days to speed them up. I will ride with you, sure. We must get ready, it's a long ride indeed, over 200 km depending on which way we go, there is a plain first, then mountains. I will analyze this at home and write later, but all this has to be carefully planned. Perhaps the best idea is to go to some small town in between Santiago and Holguín and stay overnight, continue the next day. In a rush now, back tomorrow. See attachment.

Here, a hug,

Manuel

-----Original Message-----
From: "Richard Grove" <writers@hidden-brookpress.com
Sent: 05/10/2009 4:36 PM
To: "Manuel León" <manuel.vl@hlg.rimed.cu>
Cc: "Kimberley Grove" <kesgrove@yahoo.ca
Subject: RE: Wonderful

manuel mi hermano you have made my heart sore with joy - (ache with joy - i did mean soar - fly with joy but i could not smile more without causing pain so sore with joy will do just fine) yes we will have to plan but don't forget the importance of flowing like a river - a very loose itinerary for this trip my friend. i plan

on stopping very regularly to take pictures
and write in my note book - i am planning
to write and publish a memoir from this
adventure. i need a free enlightening time
to unshackle me from the last year of hard
work. yes we can stay in a town on the way
there - maybe two or three nights if god
has that plan. i just talked to doogla and
invited him to come but he is bound by
responsibilities that will keep him here
this time. maybe - if the divine lets us
plan we can do a special trip with our
brother some other time. i am smiling at
the idea of the three of us in an old
Russian Lada heading to la habana for a
poetry conference taking the long way to get
there - dream my friend. without a dream
nothing is possible.

i am CCing kim so that she knows you will
come with me - it will lift the burden from
her heavy shoulders - my dear worrier. i
have already talked to kim's sister - a
christian science practitioner - a dear
woman - that will pray for us before we
even go and pray for us while we are
travelling. i am already praying to know
our inviolable harmony.

how long do you think you will be able to
spend with me. 3 weeks my friend??? i am
just kidding my brother. be with me on the
road for as little or as long as you can
humanly be with me. you know i am
resourceful and will survive on my own. i
have been looking at maps and have wondered

about taking the long way to santiago and biking along the coast. it would add many many klm to the trip but would be stupendous i am sure. i will have to take your advice on these matters my friend.

i am going to go to a bike shop to buy a carrier that will fit over my back wheel so that i don't have to have much on my back. i will buy one for you too. do you have a front basket for your bike? how are your tires? should i be bringing you new tires - what size? my only human worry about this trip is water. how much water will this fat old man need to carry? i don't know if i told you but i lost 20lb in the last 3-4 months. i was inspired by doogla eating protein bars and how slim he is looking - i will bring enough for both of us. i will come back from this trip heavier - more muscle.

there is more for us to talk about mi amigo but for now i am soaring with delight.

hasta pronto

adiós

su hermano

-----Original Message-----
From: "Sandi McConnell" <gotravel@bellnet.ca>
Sent: 05/10/2009 8:39 PM
To: "Richard Grove" <writers@hidden-brookpress.com
Subject: Cuba November

Good evening Richard
Sorry for the delay, I have been having trouble sending mail out today.

You are all booked.

The details: All depart Nov 27 and return Dec 4 except for you - Dec 25.

You are staying at the 4* Brisas Guardalavaca in a Villa Garden View room. Your bicycle can be your second bag at a cost of $40.00 or if you are taking two bags it will cost $75.00. The bike needs to be in a bike bag or box. Max size is 62 inches(length + width + height) and bags must not exceed 50 lbs.

You will probably want to stay in Toronto the night before as your flight is at 11:50 am, but we can talk about that later.

Let me know if you have any questions...I will send the e-ticket tomorrow.

Sandi

```
-----Original Message-----
From: "Richard Grove" <writers@hidden-
brookpress.com
Sent: 05/10/2009 11:12 PM
To: "Manuel León" <manuel.vl@hlg.rimed.cu>
Subject: FW: Cuba November
```

hello my brother

so our flight is now booked and i am already excited. i leave from cuba for home on christmas day - i will be able to spend part of the day with you my friend i will find out what time my departure is later. for now i am just happy to have this trip planned. tell my sister i will have my feet under your table soon.

i was out on my bike today - a bit of training. it is very flat here - very different from the mountains of cuba but if we take it slow and don't rush we will be fine i am sure. you are in much better shape than me. i will have to try to keep up to you.

all the best

tai

    -----Original Message-----
    From: "Manuel León" <manuel.vl@hlg.rimed.cu>
    Sent: 06/10/2009 2:35 PM
    To:"RichardGrove@spamarrest.com"
    <RichardGrove@spamarrest.com
    Subject: Those

    Hermano,

    I was reading your email and laughing with
    joy. I was noticeably moved. People around
    looked at me (it's a computers lab) and did
    not understand, just smiled kindly. Adonay
    suggests we go to Guardalavaca this time
    instead of Santiago. It would take us a
    day's ride just to go, another to return and
    there would be a lot of adventure in it.
    There are very beautiful landscapes along
    the road, she says, we can take by dust
    roads that go to hidden places in the hills
    where people live almost like when Columbus
    came, find unexplored beaches by the
    seashore, there are unexplored hills and
    caves there. When she was studying geography
    at the university, they toured the hilly
    country all along the coast to Guardalavaca,
    slept in the open, etc. She says that
    Santiago is too far for the first adventure
    and that we can hurt ourselves with unusual
    exercise. I told her that I was with you
    whatever the map, whatever the itinerary.
    She waved her head and said, "You two are a
    couple of crazy poets", though she was
    smiling and I saw the light of understanding
    in her eyes. Again, I am with you in this
    or that. I will check the size of the tiers

and no, I don't have a front basket though there is a seat for a light backpack at the back of the bicycle. One of the things we have to figure out is how to bring the bicycles back, if finally Santiago is the destination.

I am very busy with lots of things in these days. Tomorrow, I will stay home working on my thesis. I am rewriting the first chapter at the suggestion of one opponent, tough work that of reorganizing ideas indeed, but necessary. I have to finish that asap and print copies of the work for the tribunal.

Those people in the picture are my friend José Ramón Fabelo Corzo and his wife, María del Carmen. They are from Matanzas and were visiting with us. José Ramón is perhaps the best known of Cuban philosopher, a man who has published dozens of books in his field. He lectures at the University of Puebla, Mexico, where he works part of the year, and does research on values and other philosophical stuff at the Instituto de Filosofía e Historia, Havana. He read my writings about values education and gave me valuable advice. In the process, we became friends. I invited him to come to our university and he was here lecturing for a week. Besides being knowledgeable and extremely articulate, he is decent, a rare occurrence in our kind, my very dear brother, a rare case indeed. So, we had a great time discussing philosophy and politics in these days. In the meantime, we escorted them around town, to Gibara, to the beach.

I am a fortunate man, Tai. Decent people are brought by Divine's gravitation law to my life. So it happened with my sons, students and friends who truly love me, Adonay, Pablo. So it happened with my hermano Richard M. Grove.

See you soon,

Manuel

-----Original Message-----
From: "Richard Grove" <writers@hiddenbrookpress.com>
Sent: 06/10/2009 6:35 PM
To: "Manuel León" <manuel.vl@hlg.rimed.cu>
Subject: RE: Those
hello my brother

tell my dear sister, Adonay, that my heart is set on Santiago. two reasons - one is that it is my destination to go there and see the city again before i take the ccla authors in February — i need to get my footing there before i take my canadian ccla friends. the other reason is that it is just far enough that it will make me wish i was in a soft bed. i had a girlfriend many years ago, that used to say to me - you men are not having fun unless you are in pain, pushing the envelope - this is likely very

true. i have not had fun for many years -
it is over due time that i pushed the
envelope a bit — what better place than on
the road in Cuba, on a bike, side by side
with a friend.

what is the worst that can happen. we will
get tired and sleep at the side of the
road. i will tell Adonay of the times that
i slept in the ditch when i was hitchhiking
across northern ontario. it was cold and
there had not been a car in what seemed
like hours. I slid down into a frozen
ditch, put my poncho on and went to sleep
out of the wind. in the middle of the
night i woke to the echoing clatter of
gunshots. i was frozen with fear as i
watched three wolves jump the ditch right
over my stiffened body where i slept, more
gunshots, yelling, crashing, clatter, heavy
foot falls. a minute later, white-gum-
bearing dogs lept the very spot that i lay
petrified and then in a moment of eternity
three men with rifles leapt the ditch
kicking gravel down into my white awe struck
face. i slowly pulled my poncho over my
head and breathed as slowly, as shallow as
i could in hopes of not being detected,
mistaken for something to be shot at. hours
passed. with dawn's breaking hour i finally
dared venture a fearful peak over wilting
weeds to see nothing but a frost covered
landscape of silver. not a house, shed or
barn was in sight, no cars, trucks or
evidence of anything other than a silver orb
moon cradled in distant trees beckoning a

morning sun of hope. i think i will be more afraid of a lizard mistaking me for something to munch on that hunted wolves but at least i will not be threatened by frost bite. i promise adonay and kim that i will not be driven by macho hormones, i am too old for that my friend. my dream is to stop, take photographs, write in my journal as often as my heart desires or tired legs demand.

doogla was telling me about a small, light weight, self inflating, mat that might make sleeping in the open just a bit more comfortable. no sleeping bag or tent, just a light rain poncho, and a sweater — maybe sweat pants. You can bet that Fidel and Che did not have much more than that in the years they prowled the mountains.

i must go my friend. i have some turkey cooking on the stove. kim is in Toronto for a couple of days so i am eating alone. i wish you could join me.
ttys
tai

-----Original Message-----
From: "Manuel León" <manuel.vl@hlg.rimed.cu>
Sent: 09/10/2009 2:33 PM
To: "RichardGrove@spamarrest.com"
<RichardGrove@spamarrest.com
Subject: Plans

Brother, all is going to be just right.
Nothing wrong is going to happen, for sure,
only that I felt I should tell you
everything that I discussed with Adonay, but
all is going to be fine, sure.

Here, the tires of my bicycle are 26 X
1.50, I hope that's enough. I don't have a
water bottle but there is a place for it in
the bike to which some bottles may fit. I'll
see that. We will need more water, anyway.
You, in particular, forget about drinking
well water on the way.

Sure, we will go to the hotel in Miriam's car
at least once while you are there.

The plans sound terrific. Almost suicidal
beautiful. We have to think about this,
anyway. We should not bike at night, though
we could start very early, the fresh hours.
Perhaps we could ask some peasant family on
the road for permission to stay close to
their house, even for a place to take a
shower, and change, buy some food or
fruit... The guerrillas did things like that
in the mountains. There is also the
possibility that we have some cold rain, it
rains very often in the Sierra and it's
December, there are cold fronts and the
like. We will need long sleeved shirts and
hats for the sunshine. I have a couple of
shirts that will do well (white shirts that
you brought me from your father) and a hat.
We will also need raincoats (I don't have
any, they are hard to find in our shops)

Have you thought of sleeping bags? a tent or some big piece of nylon to place over our heads at night if it starts to rain?

Today, Adonay will meet a friend of ours to discuss ideas she has for her thesis. He is a very talented geographer and she will ask him about the best ideas for a route for our trip. Because Adonay is a geographer she has maps.

I will have to take some days from my job. That, I have to organize when we finally decide on precise dates. We will include a weekend in the middle, so perhaps leaving Thursday or Friday and returning Monday or Tuesday, something like that will make it easier.

I will also check on the trains if they have the possibility to help us return the bicycles to Holguin (perhaps with us). Their record in "losing" packages is infamous but that is an option. Buses will refuse, I think. There are also trucks connecting town to town to which we can probably hang the bikes. There must be ways.

Great, we will go to Father's farm. Yes, we can go on the bicycles. In the worst years of the crises (worst?) when I weighed 140 pounds, I went on my old and heavy Chinese bicycle to the farm, by the bumpy roads you know, to bring some food that saved the life of my children. We will surely go, stay overnight and come back the next day.

It's your style that compares with Hemingway's! :-)

I almost forgot, have you booked at Martha's? They are always busy and have regular visitors, etc.
Looking forward to what the Divine brings for us, my brother, all good for spiritual growth and wealth of the soul, sure,
Love from Adonay and Pablo,

Manuel

-----Original Message-----
From: "Richard Grove" <writers@hiddenbrookpress.com>
Sent: 10/10/2009 1:42 AM
To: "Manuel León" <manuel.vl@hlg.rimed.cu>
Subject: RE: Plans
hello my brother

almost fifteen hours has passed sitting at my computer. i do this too often. when so much time has passed and i can't remember what day it is let alone if i replied to you it means it is overdue time for bed or a walk on the beach. i did get out to pick up my bike from having new handle bars. even though it is 1 am i will go for a quick ride to get rid of the cob webs so i sleep better.

i have purchased a rain poncho for you. it is not fun to be wet and cold. i have to

find a hat that is good for biking or i
guess maybe i should wear my helmet.

i hope it is not a problem for you to take
time off of work. what days are best for
you. 2- 3 nights on the road and 2- 3
nights in santiago over a weekend would be
fine. i will arrive in holguin on friday
the 4th. maybe we can leave on the bikes
on thursday morning the 10th very early just
before day breaks. and be back in holguin
on tue night the 15th. does that work for
you? and your work? and your wife? :-)
we will take a bus back to holguin - they
can take our bikes in the bottom - can we
tip - it would be good to take them with us
in sight - your bike is worth $1,200.00 and
mine is worth $500.00 with my new gears.
if we let them out of our sight will we
ever see them again? i am fine with taking
a truck. just another adventure. sometimes
a tip will take one a long way.

how far is it by bike - how many hours to
your father's farm. can we stay the night?
if we go on the week 18th / 19th you will
not miss any work. how much will it cost if
i pay for a car to take adonay and Pablo to
meet us there?

i just emailed Ruben and Marta and CCed you.
now that we have talked about schedule we
can maybe tell them some dates but i can't
afford to pay for nights that i am not
sleeping there even if i lose the room -
there are other rooms - no problem.

tell my pablo that i have a hug for him
soon and my sister that the juice brother is
coming :-)

hugs

tai

-----Original Message-----
From: ""Manuel León"
<manuel.vl@hlg.rimed.cu>
Sent: 15/10/2009 1:54 PM
To: "RichardGrove@spamarrest.com"
<RichardGrove@spamarrest.com
Subject: Thank you

Thank you, in advance, amigo mío. Yes, Oct
18, this Sunday. Thank you for remembering.
There must be something special, at least a
pork steak and a small cake. Adonay must be
working on that in secrecy. We will drink
with soda to our health and wellbeing.
Right, we will pedal together to Santiago,
sure.
Back later,

Manuel

-----Original Message-----
From: "Richard Grove" <writers@hiddenbrookpress.com>
Sent: 15/10/2009 10:11 PM
To: "Manuel León" <manuel.vl@hlg.rimed.cu>
Subject: RE: Thank you

brother, yes october 18th is a special day.
you turn 35 in heart i am sure. i only
figured out right now that we are past
middle age man, 56 is when some are
looking back or fearing the next ten years.
the last stab at life before retirement. is
that what is behind this idea of mine to
bike to santiago. just an over the hill
man's last stab at life. not a last stab i
hope but one more stab.   at least i am
smart enough to know that i should not try
to bike from havana to holguin but not smart
enough to take a bus from Holguín to
santiago. god bless you for your
willingness to take a stab with me my
friend. it will be more than a foot note.
more than a paragraph. see foot note 126
manuel's 5 year old son is wondering why his
daddy is getting up so early on a weekday
and heading off with uncle tai before even
the roosters are crowing   foot note 127
tai and manuel spurred on by an aging stab
at youth straddled their bikes heading
towards santiago to soak their saddlewarn
butts in the salt waters of eternity. foot
note 172 manuel is negotiating with a truck
driver to transport tai and him with two
bikes back to holguin where adonay will
sooth their sunburned necks. i will have a
shower in your new bathroom my friend. a
new bathroom is your footnote worthy of
note.
maybe we don't need to go on this bike ride
my friend. maybe we will just sit in the
shade of a tall tree, a tip of rum, on the
dry red earth of cuba and then just make up
the entire trip. neither of us drink rum

so i guess we had better bike to santiago.
we need to tell pablo that we really did
go. we really did take the plunge in the
salt waters of eternity off the coast of
santiago and looked life straight in the
eye and said eternity can wait a while
longer while we smell the roses.

just planning this trip has been good for
me. for the first time in the years that i
have lived here i biked to downtown - only
10 kl. 25 minutes one way - flat land here
but i had never done that before.

have a good day my friend.

tai

-----Original Message-----
From: "Manuel León" <manuel.vl@hlg.rimed.cu>
Sent: 19/10/2009 5:22 PM
To: "RichardGrove@spamarrest.com"
<RichardGrove@spamarrest.com>
Subject: Late

My brother,

This portable email refused to work, perhaps
it was damaged, perhaps it's this lab,
nobody knows. So, I will use this cranky
email they provide us with, hope you
receive my email. It's late, I have been in
a meeting most of the afternoon and I am
very tired. I worked through the weekend on
my academic research, with only a moment of

rest to play with Pablo or to have a small
party with a cake (that you, again, bought
for me, thank you!) and my sister who came
to see me. I will send a photo later, sure.
Just a brief note, I have to go home before
the rain (we have been having plenty in
these days) and, again, it's quite late.
Nevertheless, there is a couple of things I
want to mention. First, I forgot your
birthday (October 7?) Adonay says she
reminded me the week before, I don't
remember her reminding me, I am so terrible
at dates, you know, but anyway, I remember
you, Pablo, Adonay, my mother every hour of
the day. And then, I forget your birthday,
Mother's birthday, and so on. I don't know
why. This is not lack of love, I just have
my mind on something elsewhere most of the
time. Adonay says that's my condition. So,
very much delayed congratulations, my
brother. You are 56, I am 57 now, I pedal
ahead and you will never reach me along the
short road of life. I pray that is so and
you and I live for some other 57 years at
least.

Yes we will go by bike to Santiago my
brother, and sleep under starry Cuban
nights, and read poetry and write under the
shade of some Sierra tree, and meet people on
the road and share a room in Santiago and
go to Santa Ifigenia Semetry where Martí
lies, and throw luck stones into the dark
waters of Stantiago bay, and find a way to
bring our bikes back by bus or truck. And
that's only the beginning of our lives.

Everything in my life began late. I found true love at 48, had Pablo at 52, wrote a scientific work on the field of my teching passion (believe me, it's truly a scientific work, whatever the tribunal determines in the end) at 55-57. And I will start life anew for my beloved and my offsprings beyond the horizon, if that is the will of God. I already understood that things under heavens organize to make my destiny what it should be just when the moment arrives. I only have to love and give, I will be loved and given in return. I will always be late, but never too late.
Love,
Manuel

-----Original Message-----
From: "Richard Grove" <writers@hiddenbrookpress.com>
Sent: 21/10/2009 11:21 PM
To: "Manuel León" <manuel.vl@hlg.rimed.cu>
Subject: RE: Late

hello my brother, your email got to me - thank youdon't worry about missing oct 7. every day is my birthday when i get to talk to you

your plans for our bicycle trip are perfect. nothing can spoil it. if we travel an inch, a mile, down into one valley and push our bikes to the top of a mountain, take a picture, write a poem and go no further the trip will be a success. the only destination i have is to be nowhere with you my brother. all we can do is head in the direction of santiago. how many palm trees we pass on the way is of no relevance. i had a dream that our bikes were tied to the side of a truck full of pigs, you and i in the cab with the driver. the stink of diesel fuel, the squealing of pigs, the noise of the grinding gears as the truck slowed as we climbed a hill, the same hill we biked down days before in the other direction. the driver let us off about 15km short of holguin and we biked the rest of the way to your home. i put my feet under your new table with pablo on my lap and had goat meat with rice and black beans cooked with onions. i am sure adonay will make that part of my dream come true. i will bring the juice

i took my bike out for a ride yesterday to find the old wild apple tree, in the park by the lake. their black, crooked arms were laden with fruit, they bowed with grace to the ground. i filled 3 bags to the brim. i wrapped the bags in my coat and took them home to make apple sauce. so very good - sweet. i wish adonay was here to help core and cook the apples, we would give some to your sons, to your sister and aunt. enough for everyone. i will pick more tomorrow. I feed the bruised and worm drilled ones to my rabbits. They hear me coming and are frantic with anticipation. hugs from brighton

tai

```
-----Original Message-----
From: "Richard Grove" <writers@hiddenbrookpress.com>
Sent: 19/11/2009 6:16 PM
To: "Eric" <////>
Subject: RE: see you soon mi amigo
```

buenos días mi amigo. what time are you arriving in holguín? you might be arriving on the very plane that is taking kim, bill and juli home - keep an eye open for them - let me know your full flight info

the likely hood is that i will not be able to meet you at the airport but a $6 to $10 cab ride will take you to my casa - come straight there. tell them to put the meter on

as soon as you have your bike and all of your luggage just wheel it outside and ask for a cab to take you to downtown holguin and show them the address for my casa.

before you leave we might have a firm place for you to stay - if not the dogs will probably not hurt you if you are sleeping in the gutter.

at the airport it is likely that there will ba a small station wagon that can take your bike.

i will be arriving at my casa the same day as you - just minutes before you. there will not be enough time for me to arrive

and then get out to the airport to greet
you. and the other problem is that they
will put the back seat down to fit your bike
so will not be enough room for me in the
cab. there is also no point in manuel
coming out to meet you for that reason. cab
drivers always speak some english - they
will take you to the casa no problem
gotta run

tai

-----Original Message-----
From: "Richard Grove" <writers@hiddenbrookpress.com>
Sent: 18/11/2009 7:34 PM
To: "Eric" <////>
Subject: RE: Cuba Trip
yowza man — great

we were planning on being on our bikes on
the way to the farm on the 19th - what time
is your flight on the 19th - saturday

we might have to just bid you farewell
before we head out. i just take a cab to the
airport. you are well travelled enough that
it will not be a problem. i have done it on
my own a few times.

i will let manuel know so he can organize a
casa for you in holguin for the days we are
there - almost a week

start looking for a box for your bike - do you have saddle bags and a water bottle

more to talk about later

ttys

tai

-----Original Message-----
From: "Richard Grove" <writers@hiddenbrookpress.com>
Sent: 16/11/2009 12:12 PM
To: "Eric" <///>; <gotravel@bellnet.ca>
Subject: Re: cuba trip nov 27

hi sandi

i would like you to meet Eric Nickerson - he is thinking of joining me in cuba for some bicycling

he is not interested in going to the resort for the week with kim, bill, juli, josh and me

can you talk to him about airfare from toronto to holguin arriving
in holguin on or after dec 3rd and leaving cuba on dec 25th or earlier

a reminder - i arrive in holguin from our resort late on dec 3rd - i leave holguin on dec 25th eric here is sandi's phone number 613-475-9842 - casa particular costs will be about $30 per night, breakfast at your casa will be about $3. my breakfast is generally large enough that i skip lunch and have dinner with your soon to be friend manuel - if we eat out dinner is max $6

we will leave dec 10th on bikes to Santiago - might stay one or two nights on the road - ditch or barn - the other nights in a casa in santiago back in holguin on tue. 15th - manuel must work on wed 16th. staying in holguin in casa 15, 16, 17, saturday 19th bike to manuel's fathers farm - one day trip or over night and bike back or truck back 21st to 25th biking locally - staying in holguin at casa.

thanks sandi

eric do you have your passport up to date
tai

-----Original Message-----
From: "Richard Grove" <writers@hiddenbrookpress.com>
Sent: 13/11/2009   10:35 AM
To: "Manuel León"
<manuel.vl@hlg.rimed.cu>"Manuel León"
<manuel.vl@hlg.rimed.cu>
Subject: RE: Eric is coming too

mi hermano - a spent some time with a very

good friend in toronto on the weekend - Eric
- i was telling him about my trip to cuba -
biking with you. next thing you know he
invited himself to come with us

he will be there from dec 5 to 19th

so it will be the three of us on the road
to santiago - it will make it harder to get
the three of us back to holguin together
with our bikes - the divine will provide the
way.

you will see he is a very special man -
also very spiritual and does not drink or
smoke. i will tell you more about him later

gotta run

tai

Hi Tai,

Sandi booked me a December 5 to 19th trip
to Holguin with Sunwing. The window of
opportunity is closing because of the close
date and popularity of XMas travel to the
area, so I grabbed it.

More later,

Eric

```
-----Original Message-----
From: "Richard Grove" <writers@hiddenbrookpress.com>
Sent: 13/11/2009   10:35 AM
To: "Manuel León"
Subject: RE: Eric is coming too
```

hello my brother

i was out for a bike ride yesterday. i had
the destination of a cemetery - i wanted to
take some pictures of some grave stones for
a book that i am doing. round trip it was
almost 35 kilometers - up and down some
hills - not mountains like in cuba - just
hills. i feel like i am getting in
condition for the trip. 35k is about 1/4
of the way to santiago i think. my mother
used to say - don't bite off more than you
can chew. i am sure we will make it
without killing ourselves. 35 k with the
hills took me about 2 hours.
This is the poem that came from that ride.

Cemetery Walk

Leaves under November-foot
crunch as I meander, camera poised
through a century of listing slabs
pitted white granite,
time-stained grey.

A distant train whistles
reminding me that time
moves on, sometimes too fast
sometimes as slow as the green
and rust-red lichen clinging,
in humble desperation.
Some try to slow or stop time
with plastic wreaths, fresh
red roses never fading
inscriptions of love chiseled
but in the end even granite
will melt into time's dusty clutches
heartfelt words
no matter how deeply carved
no matter how deeply felt
will forever be forgotten.

```
i am so looking forward to seeing you. i
have to look for a rear reflector and a
head light for our bikes.

all the best

tai
```

Foreword

My wife Kim and I have been going to Cuba for over 15 years. We started going simply because our travel agent got us a cheap package deal to an all-inclusive resort in Guardalavaca. If that trip had taken us to the Dominican Republic or Jamaica my life may have turned out quite differently. On that first trip we fell in love with the land, the sea and the beaches but most importantly we fell in love with the generous-natured people. Over time I made literary connections that led to me being invited to do workshops, readings, book launches and presentations as well as tv and radio interviews. All of these activities led me to publish the first Hidden Brook Press poetry book in English / Spanish entitled "Intimate Stranger" in 2004. That book was launched in Holguín the following year.

    I have written a couple of short Cuba memoirs in the past – "From Cross Hill" and a book of poems entitled, "A Trip to Banes". While this memoir is meant to cover a specific event – a bike trip from Holguín to Santiago de Cuba December 2009, it does describe other side trips of the same year and does hearken back to other locales, trips and sometimes even drifts into general observations about Cuba, its politics and its people. While on occasion I do tend to rant a bit about pot holes and poverty I do try to maintain an unbiased observer perspective.

I have to admit up front that I am unabashedly a Latin-American, political history neophyte – in fact maybe even a history neophyte in general. Every trip I seem to learn a bit more about the history of Cuba, its politics, its people and its three-war struggle for independence. This growing historic and sociological slant has started to shape my perspective and skew my judgments and opinions of the present. Generally, I would say that I tend to be more interested in people and their art and culture of today rather than the past but I am growing to realize that the present can hardly be seen, let alone understood, without looking though the sun-glared, time-stained window of the past. The one thing I have going for me is a willingness to ask questions, a love of people and an observant eye. I can't always promise to tell it as it is but I can always promise to tell how I see it.

Arriving

Friday, November 27th, 2009, we arrived in Holguín after a beautifully clear, almost cloudless flight.

>   submerged echo
>   cloud shadows slither
>   ocean rippling depths

On this trip, the first Spanish word for me to learn is *bicicleta* – bicycle. My Spanish is very limited but I should be able to remember this one new word. *Mi bicicleta* is now assembled in the weak air-conditioned atmosphere of our so called four-star resort of Brisas Guardalavaca. Kim and I had a rather large and bright room with a balcony side-view of the ocean. I complained right away about the weak a/c – and to my surprise a repairman came to fix it within an hour though he left for lunch soon after arriving. On return he tinkered for a few minutes, replaced the ceiling tiles and announced it was fixed. In reality it was no better after his departure. I think that this is just the little Cuban dance they do for the tourists. I suggest that in their minds the pretence of fixing something is just as good as fixing it though he seemed to know what he was doing and also seemed sincere enough in his endeavour.

I can't believe for one second that the previous occupants of the room did not find the strength of the a/c too weak though if they were like our friends Bill and Juli, in the adjacent room, the strength of the a/c was of no consequence as they never had it turned on. I, on the other hand, was grossly disappointed – but this is a diversion not worth my going into here. A memoir that I won't bother writing could be called "My Disappointing A/C Experiences of Life" as I must have plenty of gripes on the topic. I will start that book, that I won't write, with our summer heat wave in Bonn, Germany where I lectured at Bonn University. Kim and I stayed on the top floor of a 3-story walkup hotel. Not only did it not have an elevator but it did not have any a/c and we had to hound managment just to get a fan.

I should start by explaining that my darling wife, Kim, and I travelled to Cuba with our longtime dear friends, Bill and Juli and their delightful four-year old son Joshua – though sometimes monster Joshua was with us – happily infrequently. The term "Monster Joshua" was coined by Josh himself, by the way.

Joshua, my little helper friend, is a delight to work with even though he managed to loosen, even drop and roll a few essential nuts off my newly assembled bike. He discovered what an Allen key is – an important part of any man's education. "They are just funny looking little screw drivers. Look uncle Tai, I made this one come right out." I heard it fall to the cool ceramic floor. "Don't worry, we don't need it." I got everything put back together with no parts left over or missing. I eventually had to convince Joshua that the job was finished and I should have the tools back. As tools are his main passion in life this was not an easy task.

I took *mi bicicleta* out for its very first Cuban spin. This first day trip was only about 30 km – 15 out and 15 back, including a few side roads that piqued my interest and led me to interesting places called, Nowhere, that often included mountain vistas and distant misty valleys; dusty grey oxen ploughing, guided straight by wide-brim-sombreroed Cubans; strutting white egrets grooming big horn cattle. I think that this was my first-ever out of Holguín ride – See my very first camcorder video "Views of My Cuba – My First Bicycle Trip" from the Brisas resort. I was delighted, actually thrilled, would be a better word to describe the short morning trip and the results of my primitive, first video. How is it possible that it took me so long, so many years, to find my way zipping through the Cuban countryside? I feel liberated. I am looking forward to the ensuing excursions though I can't help wonder how the technology of a digital camcorder altered my experience. Peering at Cuba through a documentary eye, no matter how naive I may be as a videographer, will be different than viewing my Cuba in "the now" without the ego of hoping that someone might like even a single frame of my video. How can one experience the existential "now" when one is thinking about the future? Because I am an artist, a writer and a publisher I was instantly, without even seeing any of my raw footage, planning to publish at least one documentary from my footage. I guess this will be my foray into the world of U-Tube. If I were not in Cuba I might have already posted it for the world to see. It will be interesting to see how this instant visual media will alter, influence my writing if at all.

Each section of the video is virtually wordless. There are the occasional distant muffled "Hola" to and from passers-by, the clop clop of horses and the rush of traffic. For the most part a grey sky hung silently heavy with moments of dragging mist that hesitated into rain.

The next day, Kim and I biked the first short leg of my yesterday's excursion into the small hamlet of poverty I had previously zipped past. A red dirt road lined by cactus hedges led us into ten or fifteen houses, maybe best described as mostly ramshackle and unkempt. Each house is typically only about twenty to twenty-five feet square, most often with a tin roof but sometimes capped with a fine palm frond thatching. The Cubans call such dirt floor houses *bohíos* though sometimes they do have some of the rooms finished with tiles laid directly on the compacted red dirt. I have been in many of both style of roofed houses – from my limited visitor perspective the tin-roofed houses seem to be so much hotter than a thatched roof house. The rain permeability of a thatched roof is not at all inferior to corrugated steel. I know many that have lived with a thatched roof all of their life and do not seem to be dripped on and worse for wear.

Over fifteen years of wondering why some Cubans do what they do has not reaped me any concrete answers though I suspect that in the case of tin compared to thatching it has to do with the slow erosion of culture. At one time every man would know how to thatch a roof. Now with the availability of corrugated steel few would know. Did the loss of skill precipitate the need of corrugated steel or was it the other way around? Did the availability of corrugated steel precipitate the loss of an ancient skill? What does it matter anyway? Well it does matter. The loss of such a simple and practical skill creates dependency. When hurricane Ike blew the roofs off many hundreds of houses many stayed roofless for years. I have seen evidence of this where years later families that had a corrugated steel roof ripped off and destroyed still do not have government, family or personal resources to buy more steel so they live roofless. It is so sad. In another era they would have rallied together as a neighbourhood and simply rebuilt with the resources that Mother Nature provided and the skill that a living culture had sustained.

Father and son in Gibara.

Women migrated from the darkness of their kitchens greeting us with shells and necklaces for only a few pesos. It was as if a TPD – tourist proximity detector – sensed our presence.

Outstretched Hands

> red dirt road
> trimmed cactus hedgerows
> mark boundaries, disobeyed
> by free-roaming chickens.
>
> women of every age tumble
> from the darkness
> of their ocean-front kitchens
> outstretched hands
> offer shells and trinkets
> toothless smile of hope retreats
> unrequited
> a young bronzed man, slender
> invites
> us into his home for coffee
> the opportunity of parallel market
> income denied
> we mount our bikes
> and quickly depart

It is not that we felt particularly unsafe. The offers of their wares were presented unhoundingly from a comfortable distance, it is just that our Canadian prosperity could only be confronted so many times in such a short period of time. If we stuck around we would have to exercise a commonly used Spanish phrase – "*no gracias.*" a few too many more times

Even though we are staying in the resort for one week the days are already starting to blend into each other – what day is it? How many more sleeps are left before we leave, floats to the top of my thinking a number of times each day.

What Day Is It?

Swim, eat, snooze, swim, eat, snooze, swim, eat, snooze, swim, snooze, eat, swim, snooze, swim, snooze, swim, eat, swim, eat, snooze, sleep.

Joshua's Version

Pool, ocean, pool, ocean, eat, resist snooze, pool, ocean, pool, ocean, eat, resist snooze, pool, ocean, pool, ocean, eat, collapse in mother's arms, sleep.

Rural Work Ethic

One day while bicycling something struck me about the rural work ethic in Cuba and why work is so often performed at such a slow pace. For years I have had some level of judgment about the seeming lack of drive and speed of accomplishing work and blamed it, at least in part, on the climate. The heat of the day would slow anyone down was the accepted rationale. As a labourer

I have worked plenty of hours sweating with one tool or another in the heat of a summer day. At least when I was a roofer, toiling, I knew the summer period would soon be finished and my heat-pounding labours would last for a maximum of three months with a couple of cooler months tacked on each end if I were not in school. Aside from the short hot work season I also knew that this labour would only last for a few years – for me roofing lasted only four seasons. With the Cubans it would be a lifetime of toiling in the heat, month after month, year after year. One would learn to pace oneself. Pacing oneself becomes a life necessity, life necessity becomes a life style, a life style over generations becomes culture, culture becomes life style and the cycle continues and is blindly self-perpetuated.

Well, back to my revelation – one day while bicycling I came upon three men shoveling sand and gravel onto an oxen cart in the heat of the late morning sun. They shoveled at a reasonable, though moderate speed. By the time I passed by again they were finished shoveling and were now perched on top of their mound plodding away at loaded-oxen-cart speed. As you can imagine high gear for a gravel-loaded oxen cart would be slow indeed. I smiled at the workers, nodded with *bueno dias* and bicycled past them to find the next leg of my adventure. Two hours later on a different road I passed them going at breakneck oxen-cart speed down a hill. I jokingly noted that this fast oxen-cart speed was not even fast enough to flutter their shirts. Once again I smiled, waved and passed by. Forty-five minutes later I was returning down the same road. This time they were going uphill at caterpillar-in-sand speed while I zipped past them at ear-whirring speed with hardly the time to smile, nod and wave. It was at this point that I had my revelation that had to do with labour mindset and the speed of transportation.

Ox Cart Plod

Oxen plod in low gear
up long hill.
Cart loaded
with laboured sand and gravel
three men perched on mound
their morning toil.
Lumbering in now noonday heat
their destination eats
at dwindling productive hours.

What is the point of scurrying to fill the cart when they will soon be perched on top plodding along to their dumping destination. The few minutes of time created by shoveling quickly would soon be eaten up by the slow speed of the transportation mode. The oxen cart was the magical dictator of their productivity not the heat of the day or their moral fiber. The heat may have a contributing factor slowing them down but not at all as much as the slow speed dictated by the oxen cart. There is not much point in shoveling quickly when more than half of their day will be spent sitting on the mound they created. Can you imagine how much faster they would have to work if there was a truck that zipped in for a load and demanded that they fill his truck as quickly as possible because the driver was getting paid for the number of loads he delivered in a day. They would soon demand a raise in pay or quit out of sheer exhaustion.

When equipment is regularly breaking down or is never working properly there is no incentive or drive to work faster. When your pay is not linked to your productivity there is no motivation to find or create a better way. When the technology dictates your speed, when resources are so limited that you can't create a better way, even if you were inspired to invent it, then there is no faster speed than slow.

To parallel this with my life, this low tech, low speed, low demand somehow feels enviable as I still after four days have not fully decompressed from the flurry of publishing that I did in the last months before coming to Cuba. My tools don't just allow but somehow demand that I be productive 24/7. It is time to take better control of my tools and be as productive as my wellbeing demands.

On that day of bicycling I was able to stop and smell the roses as it were, in this case smell the grasses. I took a few short videos of swaying grass. I was inspired by the gentle undulations of the soft grass as it waved back and forth. I will edit them into a meditative film sometime when I get home – if I can find the time.

Eternal Hope

Swaying in breeze
of eternal hope
century old roots
of resilience
reach deep
to Soul's expectation
that all is well.
"The grass beneath our feet,
silently exclaims
The meek shall
inherit the earth." [1]

[1] – *Science and Health by Mary Baker Eddy p. 516:12*

Moving to Holguín

Thank heavens the resort part of the trip is finished. It is Saturday the 5th – 20 days before Christmas. The beach-time-lazy-hours are fine for a few days, but my soul soon starts to long for adventure. Kim, Bill, Juli and Josh have gone home now and I have moved from the resort to *mi casa* in Holguín – I will miss them but without them it is very much a different type of trip. I have stayed in this casa a couple of times in the past. One thing I like is the large outdoor dining table where I have my breakfast and set up my laptop to do my morning writing and editing. Eric, *mi amigo de* Toronto will arrive later in the day. His *casa* was pre arranged by Martha and Ruben, the owners of *mi casa*, and will be only two houses from where I am staying.

* * *

Eric has moved in and has been coming over about 8 am each morning for breakfast – *el desayuno*. This year I have curbed eating greasy foods as much as possible so have not had eggs and ham - *huevo y jamón* at *mi casa* as I have previous years. Buns, cheese, fruit, orange juice and coffee stretched over a couple of hours of writing is working very well for me. As was the case with other years I find this to be a very productive time of the day. After breakfast Eric goes off to explore the city and returns in time for a siesta and a bike ride to Manuel, Adonay and Pablo's place for a visit, walk, dinner, coffee etc. My daily visit with Manuel, my Cuban brother, *mi hermano*, is a joy that makes the trip special.

Today, December 8th, Eric and I sat in a flowering-vine-draped café having a soda while we chatted to a couple from England. An older woman approached each of us, methodically, one at a time pestering us for un peso. None of us succumbed to her persistence, though I know I have given to her in the past, a number of times in fact. Such a face I could hardly forget.

Richard M. Grove

Origami for the Beggar Lady

A beggar lady planted herself at my feet
leaned on my table with deliberation and looked
me straight in the eye with outstretched hand.
She mumbled something to me
in Spanish that included the word peso.
Her freckled, wrinkled brow creased
the intensity of time, her ghost-blue eyes
told me this was her full-time occupation.
I didn't have a single "no" left in me.
I couldn't find the energy to tell her
I had no pesos for her, Cuban or Convertible.
Reaching into my bag I pulled
out a pen and drew a smiley face on a greasy
slip of paper that was previously my
cinco-peso-pizza-pinch-paper.
I folded it slowly with precision
every motion carefully watched
I placed it gently in her hand
and looked away.
She unfolded the paper slowly
even though she knew what was on it.
She looked at it quizzically
then looking at me she smiled,
put the paper on the table and slid
it back to me. She held out her hand again.
I pulled the paper to me and drew
another smiley face, folded it again
with the same precision

I put it in her outstretched hand.
On sliding it back to me the second time
I drew a third smiley face, folded it
once again and put it gently in her hand.
With a calm sense of anticipation she unfolded
the paper, examined it, smiled
an even bigger smile
this time, finally, she slid it back to me
and walked away.

December 09 / 09

It was sunny and very hot. I would guess 32 – 35 °c. I moved slowly up the street zigzagging from shade to shade. I was drawn to the sound of children playing in the distance.

Enthusiasm

I stopped at the school yard fence
in the belching heat of a Cuban afternoon
drawn close by cheers and jeers
of adolescent competition.
Skins and shirts battle
with chest-thumping pride
strutted, paraded to
arm flailing, bouncing pubescent

cheer leaders, hyped.
Thub, thub, a partially inflated
soccer ball leaves the toe
of one champion to the chest
of his adversary.
There is nothing un-inflated
about their enthusiasm.

Santiago de Cuba Departure

Thursday we rose at 4:30 am, breakfast at 5 am. Loaded our bikes by 5:45 am, straddled them by 6 am. We had a long city departure. Holguín stretches for many miles from the downtown. It seemed to take forever to get beyond the city limits into the calm of country. My first thrill of the trip was the silver morning mist that enveloped the landscape. Everything was swallowed by green grey. The morning melted into 32 °c by 11am. Outside of Holguín, the hills started to grow and test our endurance. By noon we were pushing our bikes up some killer hills. The forever optimist in me saw the bike pushing hills as either the opportunity for a good view or the opportunity to coast down at full breathtaking, shirt-drying speed. Only once on the first day did I wonder, why the heck, I was there. The rest of the time, despite some bike-eater hills, I was always glad I was on the trip.

Over Coming Hills

The valleys we left behind
the mountains before us
so breathtaking
I give body little consideration.
When the mind is full of beauty
body utters no complaints.
Only from time to time
between royal palms and sky
twinges of body try to drag me
into thinking I am mortal.
Any drudgery of staring
at sweat-dripped pavement while we,
in slow motion, climb a hill
is surpassed by ecstasy
of a face-to-sky glide.

It is a miracle of overcoming matter to think that we glided on wings of joy, down far more mountains than we trudged up. How is it possible that there are more downs than there are ups?

The Sugarcane Juice Booth

I will return later to other special moments of the day but at this instant, I am thinking about mid-afternoon and arriving at the sugar cane juice booth. We had bicycled all day through glorious mountains and valleys, stunned by magnificent vistas. By the afternoon we were relieved from pedalling up hills for a while when we plateaued onto the brilliant green, flat swaths of sugarcane fields of Loynaz Hechevarría. After tens of miles and miles and miles bordered by eight-foot tall sugar cane we came upon a bus stop area that seemed to be situated somewhere between nowhere and somewhere else. This is where the sugar cane juice-squeezing booth – a rustic, ten foot by ten foot rebar structure with a tin roof – was situated. It was quite literally out in the middle of nowhere. The mountains that we were heading towards were off in the distance some 40 or 50 miles away. The last town that we had passed was in the hills about 20 miles back and we had not passed any crossroads since then. All there was was a vast wash of green and we were right in the middle of it. There were a few shabby small trees along the road here and there. Other than that it was green sugarcane everywhere one looked – amazing.

I was taken by the marvelous simplicity of running eight-foot lengths of sugarcane through a simple rolling press and being served a frothing cup full of *"Guarapo"* – sugar cane juice. To my surprise, the guarapo was more like food than sugar water. It was sweet but not like cola. It was more like drinking a room temperature ice cream float – smooth. I wonder if there is a north American market for canned guarapo. The cane was run through the press three times, the second and third time twisted like a damp rag to glean more of the golden juice. A large dented aluminum mug of guarapo cost about five Canadian cents. The wrung-out sugarcane was piled to the side.

I could not help but wonder what value might be

found in the thousands or millions of tons of spent sugarcane the country must produce annually. Can the fiber be broken down for paper use, insulation, some kind of fuel pellets like for a wood pellet stove, glued into pressboard etc.? I have no idea if they use if for anything – I would like to know. Do they burn it or I hope at least compost it? I wonder if my Havana scientist friend Bruno would know.

After our guarapo we moved over to a concrete bus shelter where Manuel made coffee, Cuban style. He had packed all of the needed ingredients and accoutrements, including an alcohol burner and espresso maker. Here we were having coffee like the Italians or French but we were in the middle of nowhere at the edge of a sugarcane plantation in Cuba. I found the juxtaposition remarkably humourous . It reminded me of movies where a rich British aristocratic family on a safari in India would stop for afternoon tea and roll out the carpets, tents and fineries. We three were aristocrats in our own way. Sipping the finest in the fresh air of Cuba without a care in the world, how perfect it was.

After a forty-five minute rest we headed back on the road – it was infernally hot – I am sure the temperature scorchingly hovered around 35 °c. The last generous stop we had had was hours earlier standing under a large green, breeze-ruffled canopy at a quiet "T" intersection. We stopped to inquire as to our location and direction to where we were headed. At his juncture there was a simple booth, vendor stand selling ham sandwiches and a papaya milk shake drink. Neither of which we timid, intestinally fragile, Canadians dared partake. I will not give you a gurgling description of the last time I boldly, unabashedly gulped such a culinary delight. I will leave my eruptive memory to your imagination. Needless to say we stuck to glugging our bottled water.

A Long Day

We had a long day of biking that ended in Mella (sounds like Maya) a bit earlier than expected. Bleary eyed we had hit the road in Holguín by 6am, we heroically conquered some major "bike-busting" hills, we rejoiced on the flat roads of the sugarcane fields, had our guarapo and coffee rest and headed off for Mella to buy needed water. The hot day left us close to the end of our water reserve and we were starting to ration. Mella was a doable distance, Palma Soriano was too far on the limited water we had. These next two hours were difficult for me with some long hills that I surrendered possibly too quickly.

Reluctantly, we took the rather long 3 km detour off the main highway into Mella. The boulevard into the town was gorgeous and cool. Moss covered trees canopied the wide street creating a cherished shady path of recovery from hours of sun. Tan faced Cubans smiled and waved to us as we entered their hidden sanctuary. A gaggle of children swarmed us as we slowed to a stop to ask for directions to a store that sold water. "The store is "close" *señor*." "Can you take us there?" Without hesitation he turned and ran in the direction of the town centre. Pedalling quickly to catch up we followed him for quite a distance. As quickly as he bolted away from us he stopped and pointed at the store. "The store is closed *senior*." Hand smacked to forehead I said "Not close but closed." Everything in town was closed because of the power blackout. The one small department store that sold bottled water had closed its doors for the day. With Manuel's help we were then directed to the only other place in the entire city that sold water – it was a large trailer-size-booth-flip-up-front type of store. We lined up and bought enough water and pop to get us by. Our purchase was likely the largest single sale of water and pop the store had ever made to one customer. We lugged out bags and bikes to a shady spot and fell onto park benches to guzzle our newly acquired booty. Our thirst was finally quenched.

It was so hot and now late in the day that we started wondering if we should be staying in Mella for the night and not press on to Palma Soriano as had been our growing expectation. The dilemma – If we stayed in Mella we would have to make up those 20km tomorrow but if we head out with our new supply of water now we will most certainly not get to Palma Soriano until after dark. Contem-plation left us with Manuel setting off looking for a place for us to stay the night. On his return we discovered there was only one *casa* available and not an official government approved *casa* particular. No electricity would mean not only no a/c but no fan. The prospect of a hot night and added 20km tomorrow added up to support our only one conclusion – move on to Palma Soriano despite how late and tired we were.

The Ride in the Big Blue Truck Story

Over the years of travelling together, Manuel and I have learned to look for, and indeed expect, divine synchronicity to unfold and solve all problems. The expectation of good is an important precept that I was taught and have tried to embrace most of my life. We have seen surprising, unexpected solutions presented to us in the past. This time our need was met by a big blue truck going to Palma Soriano. It could take our bikes and the three of us for the 20 km ride – the fee? – 4 CUC for Eric and 4 CUC for me. Manuel and his bike would ride for free as a Cuban. What a great solution – under $10 CND to be delivered not only in our direction but to the city of our original destination. The ride was a standup thrill of a breeze. I have had many thrills this trip but this one takes the sugar cane.

There was a waist-high railing for us to lean our bikes on, and hold on for dear life once we were streaming down the highway. As soon as our bikes were in place and we were settled for takeoff, Cubans started to pile into the truck with us. We did not see the driver receiving any payment for these passengers. Our only conclusion was that he normally drove that route and was only charging us Canadians the 8 CUC payment for the ride. By the time we were leaving Mella we had 15 more people in the truck with us. As we stopped part way down the highway to let people off more piled on. Duffle bags, shopping bags, purses, one after the other would appear over the edge, tossed 8.5 - 9 feet in the air, followed by smiling Cuban faces, scrambling hand over hand. Hair whipped in the heat of the now early evening, we barreled down the highway. Everyone was joyously pleased to have an effortless ride. With a sharp whistle or bang on the roof of the truck we would come to a quick stop. While one or more piled off three or ten would pile on. Always tossing a bag in with faith that they would be able to scramble, clamber on before the big blue boat sailed off without them. More than once a bag was tossed off to the stranded person that did not make the scrambling clamber to the steel deck. Forlorn they were left in the dust waiting for the next possible transport salvation.

It was on this trip that I finally learned how to dance, though maybe not to any standards that would please Kim. I call my new dance "the blue-truck-oil-slick shuffle." As we later discovered, this truck had been used to transport barrels of vegetable oil. The evidence glistened over the steel floor and coated the railings. There was no sitting or leaning on this trip, unless you wanted oil stain blotches on your clothes. This mode of people transport is very common in Cuba. Open work trucks that normally carry gravel, sand, lumber etc. will carry people in off work hours. It is a wonderfully serendipitous way of travelling. One in the need of a ride could hardly be expected to turn it down but in this age of seatbelts and air bags it could hardly be considered safe but then again safety is the least of worries for a foot-weary Cuban traveller simply wanting to get home for dinner.

A Memorable Face

On this trip there were many memorable faces but there was one old man in particular who sticks in my mind. He had a wrinkled mahogany, sun-patinaed face of joy. His gentle presence exuded kindness and a willingness to connect to the heart. He didn't have to say a word to say hello. Between a bit of my broken Spanish and his broken English we spoke of *mi bicicleta* and our trip from Holguín. He laughed and said this truck ride is giving my bike a needed rest. He graspingly clutched the steel railing as we lurched forward heading back onto the highway. When we reached wind-swept speeds I noticed his hat starting to flutter. I patted him on the top of his hat. His smile and nod was his gracious, brotherly reply of gratitude. Without words he knew I was worried that his straw hat, his *sombrero*, might flap off in the wind and be left, a dot on the dusty road. On his departure he patted me on the shoulder and said "have a good afternoon, *buenos tardes mi amigo*." He spryly leapt over the railing, one foot on the slippery ladder, skipping three rungs he jumped to the ground, a wave to me, a sharp whistle to the driver and he was gone from my life forever. He asked for nothing, I gave him nothing other than a pat on his hat. I did not know his name but I will always remember his deep smile. A grandfather I never had, an ambassador of international relations disappeared in the dust with one hand still in the air waving.

That moment and many more like it are what cemented this trip as a voyage from person to person.

This trip has been more about people than maybe any other trip I have ever had. Moments like these are what cause a trip to be more than just an average life experience about place. I have been lucky enough to have had many similar experiences over the years.

I am reminded of a time in Canada when I took a picture for a beer-bottle collector redneck and his wife on their honeymoon. An hour-long chat at Kakabeka Falls told me that this young man was more than just a beer bellied redneck. The generosity of spirit that he had for his wife and others left a marked impression on me.

I am reminded of the truck driver who picked me up at 3 am at the crossroads to nowhere on my way to Fort McMurry. He told me in few words how much he loved his son. He showed me the mottled black and white mutt of a puppy he had in a box and told me how far he had to drive to pick it up. He had been on the road for five days and sadly missed the birthday party. Between all of my travels in New Zealand, Germany, France, England and further I have never had so many wonderful people-times as in Cuba. Travelling from friend to new friend, to strangers who became friends has been heartwarming.

Arriving in Palma Soriano

On our arrival at Palma Soriano, in the famous blue grease truck, we hoisted our bikes over the slippery railing to the street. I made adjustments to my chain and with now black greasy fingers headed off looking for a *casa particular* for the night. Once again, thank heavens for Manuel – after chatting with a few local Cubans he trundled off looking for a certain Alexander who apparently had rooms for rent in his "registered" *casa*. Good news / bad news – Forty-five minutes later Manuel returned to the main square, where he left Eric and me, with the news that he found an Alexander who rented cars, not rooms, to tourists. The lucky news is that this first Alexander directed him to the second Alexander with rooms for rent. Because of the expected distance Manuel needed his bike as it was more than a few blocks away. He headed off with our hopes, our dreams for a comfortable bed, safely gliding under the sureness of his speedy wheels.

Good news / bad news – Another forty–five minutes later he returned and said there were three rooms now reserved for us but two of the rooms were being used by local Cubans – rented by the hour – if you get my drift. By now it was getting dark. Street lights were blinking on, stores were closing and once again musicians were starting to drift to the parks. Cuba, the chameleon, was once again changing its colours from the light and bright, breeze-filled-palm-swaying, children playing, island to the dark and mysterious, soulful music capital of the world. Soon the main square would be overflowing with toe tapping, hip swaying gyrations of salsa and rumba.

The Sleeping in the Brothel Story

As there appeared to be very few options in this non-tourist town, we headed off with our trusty Manuel in the lead to find this infamous house – a private *posada* – that we quickly dubbed "the brothel." We arrived through dark quiet streets gently gliding in, out and around the usual, often large, potholes. We pulled up to a rather capacious house with stunning blue double doors at the side where we would enter with our bikes. After maneuvering in this side entrance, guarded by two small, hyper-active, very yappy dogs, we were shown to the one, presently available room. As is always the case with registered *casa particulars* the room was large with a private floor-and-wall-tiled bathroom and a cool-pumping air conditioner. By now it was 8 pm and we decided to have a shrimp and pasta dinner on the roof while we waited for the other two "presently occupied" rooms to be vacated.

Dinner on the roof was delightful. The gentle orange glow of incandescent moons only partly obscured the view to the dazzling sky. Here we were, less than two weeks before Christmas, in our brothel of choice, called heaven, with the wafting aroma of shrimp and parmesan cheese filling the swaying-palm-tree-view third floor patio. The gentle click, click of dominos echoed in the moonlit street below, followed by jovial cheers of victory and defeat. Crepuscular residence flowed into the cool streets with music spilling from a CD player tethered by electric cords dangling from the living room window. It was a long day and all was relaxingly perfect. The yapping dogs downstairs had finally calmed down and were snoozing nose to nose. The hot day was melting from under us—that is until the glorious cool breeze was filled with the acrid odour of burning wires and the pop popping of light bulbs interrupted our dinner. We were plunged into darkness. Alexander came rushing, followed by his wife, followed by the staff, followed by the yapping dogs. "Where is the fire?" bellowed Alexander as smoke billowed. We presumed by the abundance of smoke that it was not just a fuse that had blown. After a few minutes of scurrying, hollering and yapping it was announced that the problem was under control but the new service wires that were just installed that day had over heated and burned out, leaving most of the house, including our dining area, in darkness. A few minutes later Alexander announced that he had already called the electric company and they were on their way but they would have limited power in the rooms and no a/c. "What does, on their way mean? In Cuba time?" I smiled. Our compensation for the flapping interruption was a few delightful candles placed or maybe rather plunked on the table. The dogs were shooed to the distant quarters of the house.

The stars in the heaven were starting to cave in. The good news was that Manuel's room was now available but my room, the third room, still had a lineup of beer swigging, neck-sucking locals waiting for their romping moment in my bed. Move over Eric. In a manly fashion Eric and I, with at least a foot between us lay on the bed in the non-air conditioned waft of a fan. Eric I love you but I want my own bed. 12:30 am eventually rolled over my weary head. Don't tell me that the lustful lineup for my room is not finished yet. I stomped "gently" out of Eric's room only to find the entire house was asleep. Not only was the line finished but the dogs and the owner were asleep and my room was locked. I was bloody well determined to have my own bed. Tip toeing like Santa looking for the Christmas tree I made my way down the long stairs to the owner's private apartment. If Santa had ever been greeted by thunderous yapping dogs the way I was he would have hung up his sack and retired long ago. I put one tip-toe on the top step and all hell broke loose. Canadian guard dogs have nothing on these yapping mutts. I learned something about yapping mutts that night – never wave a bare toe in their direction thinking you are going to shoo them into quiet submission. The pitch got louder and the incessant yapping turned to teeth-gnashing growls. Thank goodness Alexander came to my rescue. Now why didn't I think to say shoosh in Spanish and snap my fingers? All was instantly quiet and the neighbourhood sighed a collective sigh. It only took two or three minutes of hand gesticulations and a bit of broken Spanish for me to be shown to my non- a/c no fan room. If Santa is smart he will bypass this house.

It was 1 am when I finally put my head on my "yes the sheets were clean" pillow. Smack, smack – hungry greedy mosquitoes had invaded my room. Within minutes I was mauled by the little buzzing stiff proboscis beggars – windows and door were open

Last Stretch Before Santiago de Cuba

Tai and Manuel

Manuel and Eric

Manuel

because of no a/c or fan. Up I get even, though in fear of waking the now vicious dogs, I tiptoe, squeak, squeak, bare feet, out of my room on cool tiles to get my bug repellent from Eric's room – I don't think I woke him – thank heavens his door was unlocked. 1:20 am I was finally sound asleep? 4:30 too soon, I found Eric at my bed side. He was not there to spoon with me but to wake me for our previously arranged very early 5 am departure. Who's idea was it to come on this damn trip anyway? A quick shower to wash off the bug spray and I was downstairs paying my bill and loading my bike. Oh, but where are the frickin' yapping dogs? I motion to Alexander with a derivative yap, yap, yap. Oh, simple. He put them in a room upstairs so they wouldn't bark. I hoped they were hanging upside down by their dew claws in the dark.

A 5 am Departure

Bills paid – I argued and paid less for my three hour sleep, saddle bags packed. Mrs. Alexander – I never knew her name – smiled as she handed over a small package of deep fried plantain – leftovers from our previous night's dinner, in the dark, on the roof. These stale, not so crisp leftovers would soon be our roadside snack. The side door was unlocked; the clatter of the sliding deadbolt echoed into the cool, still street, our bikes rattled down the single step to the damp pavement. The black of 5:05 am greeted us like strangers – skinny skulking Cuban dogs dashing past the long beam of light cast to the street. We whispered our way out of the city. It was cool, like an August summer morning in Ontario. Mist hung in the trees. Our bikes traced dew glistening lines on the damp road as we disappeared leaving Palma Soriano in the distance. The air was tranquil, still. This was a silent magical time pedalling into nowhere, a ghostly mist gathering on my arms shimmering in the moonlight. Within a few minutes we reached the highway. The ramp took us to our fated south. Santiago de Cuba was within morning striking distance if the slopes of the mountain barrier were not too daunting – we would soon find out.

For the first hour or more we peddled up hill, in the dark, at a slow disheartening pace. Distance grew between us, the leader stopping from time to time to let the others catch up; moral support is essential when faced with the push of a hill in the dark. Your mind wanders, you can easily pick up speed or slow to a crawl when you only have the faint glow of a headlamp following a solid white line. The metronome of your heart sets your pace. Even if you are in the right gear your mind, in a visual void, gets tired before your muscles. If nothing, it was an exhilarating experience, pumping in the dark. Bicycling in the quiet cool was a thrill that I could not have anticipated.

The distant mountains and palm-lined highway woke gently before us. First the morning mist started to glow an eerie silver and then thinned ever so slowly as the sun rose. By the time we had light enough to read road signs we had about 30 km left before we would see Santiago. We were on the main three lane highway with the middle lane as the right-of-way for uphill passing. We had biked up some pretty long, arduous hills this morning. By 8:30 am the clear-blue-sky temperatures had already risen into the high twenties. We were tired and hungry after 3.5 hours of steady slogging. Protein bars while pedalling and water can only carry you so far. It was time for a special Manuel-style coffee break.

The Coffee In the Ditch Story

Considering we had been on the road and uphill since 5 am we decided that it was overdue time for a coffee break. By this time we were in a steady stream of traffic. Sometime in the dark hours of the morning the highway had moved into four lanes, two in both directions with a groomed and flowered medium between. We found a shady spot down in a grassy ditch beside a sugarcane plantation. Manuel broke out his coffee kit while I headed into the lush green, with TP in hand, to visit "Mother Nature," if you know what I mean. The cane field is a mysterious close-knit place. The plants are over eight feet tall and planted very close together with long sharp leaves. Have you ever been in the middle of a corn field in late summer and all you can see is green? The claustrophobic feeling of lost and trapped is much the same. You have to move slowly and sure footed so you are not chaffed by serrated leaves. The sheer density makes it almost impossible to move other than at a slow defensive pace. The sugarcane rows are planted much closer together than corn and let in even less light. This is not a field that one would play hide and seek in. Within very few minutes one would find themselves lost with no clue as to east or west.

With a few minutes of shut eye after Manuel's *café negro* elixir and another protein bar we halfheartedly dragged ourselves back to our bikes. By now the pavement was furiously hot but our spirits soured as soon as we picked up speed and glided through the silver curtains of heat that shimmered in our path. Only one more long hill and we would be heading down into Santiago. On this long perfectly paved potholeless highway we had a wide clear shoulder to continue our uphill push towards the mountains. If it had not been for the stupendous views we would have been disheartened by the many hour-long climbs. We gazed over valley-stretching bridges to the tops of swaying Royal Palms nodding, eye to eye, to kiting vultures. Then finally we were at the top.

I will have to consult a topographical map for accuracy but it seemed that we were headed down with no more ups somewhere around 20 – 25 km without a single painful peddle push – what a thrill. The mountains slid silently under our feet into the cool azul ocean below. We stopped a few times amid the massive walls simply to take in the astonishing views and click a few pictures. I made up a simple song as we zipped the last leg of our trip. I was singing at full volume at full tilt for this last stretch.

Eric and Manuel - coffee in the ditch.

Eric and Manuel - coffee in the ditch.

Eric and Manuel - a minor repair.

Manuel and Eric looking at the statue.

Antonio Maceo Revolution Square.

Santiago de Cuba looking to the harbour.

A Santiago rooftop.

Arriving in Santiago de Cuba

Santiago here we come
Santiago here we come
The morning mist is all around
The sliver moon she's hanging high

Santiago is calling us
The highway they made straight and strong
A few more minutes gliding down,
Santiago here we come.

Santiago there you are
The gorgeous mountains parted wide
The Royal Palms they cheer us on
Santiago de Cuba here we are.

For well over an hour we glided effortlessly down into the city arriving at the breathtaking view of Antonio Maceo Revolution Square. We pulled our bikes up onto the sidewalk and stood in awe at the inspiringly humungous statue of Antonio Maceo glancing behind him, one hand raised, waving his troops into battle, 16 meters in height, the tallest statue in the whole country. The front feet of his stallion were raised triumphantly in the air indicating that this brave leader died in battle. Did you know that tradition has it that if the statue of a cavalry leader has all four legs of his horse on the ground that it symbolizes that he died in bed of non-battle related causes? Further to tradition, if his horse has one front foot in the air it symbolizes he died later in bed but from wounds sustained in battle. After our inspiring arrival, our middle-aged triumph, we humbly crossed the street pushing our bicycles, dodging noon rush hour traffic. Even though we had just arrived we headed into the bus terminal conveniently located right in front of us to inquire about our departure times, four days from then. These middle-aged men were after all taking the bus back to Holguín. None of us particularly wanted to have the statue of us erected with the front wheel of our bike raised in the air.

I am standing on the roof of Maria Elena's house looking up hill.

Coffee on the Roof

Yesterday Eric and I had coffee on the roof of our new *hermana* – sister – Maria Elena's *casa* in Santiago de Cuba – such a time of camaraderie. "We are moving in the economy of affection," said *mi amigo / mi hermano* Eric / Enrique. We sat in the shade of Maria Elena's simple, unadorned cement platform roof talking, not talking, staring at the Cuban sky, the hillside wall of cascading houses, the rich natural textures, the cobbled houses, the trees and plants that eeked a living from corners and crannies fed by sun. Our time together for those four days was as rich as the scene that enveloped us.

    Maria Elena's daughter, Cristina, a calm sixteen-year-old with a sincere aspiration of becoming an artist, and I sat on this roof of inspiration and drew a few times. I was intimidated by her enthusiasm and my decades-long drought of not drawing seriously. I made a contract with her that if she drew 25 pictures of that rooftop scene I would buy two of them for 10 CUC when I returned in a few weeks at the end of January. One evening we reclined looking at shooting stars – *las shooting estrellas*. In Ontario our shooting star period is in mid august, if I remember correctly, but here it was announced in the news for that night. The sky was clear and filled with sparkling mythological gods of a different era. Silence and the burning tales that lasted a millisecond bonded us as nothing else could.

A White Chalk Line Marked Her Past

A woman turned the corner in front of me.
I could hear her grinding approach
for blocks before she finally came in sight.
She was dragging what was once
a trundle buggy – a handle with two wheels
a wire box for groceries.

Hers was almost unrecognizable as such.
The wire box was long gone,
one wheel was missing, replaced
with an aluminum hub
a wheel of some other sort,
it did not turn anymore. The other wheel
was missing altogether.

What still made it a trundle buggy
was the handle to which a bundle was strapped.
As it dragged
along the street it rumbled, grinding
a white chalk line.

It marking her path
a stick-dragged beach.
Everyone knew she was coming,
everyone knew she had passed.

Sunday Morning On The Front Porch of Roberto's Casa

In Cuba, symbols of poverty pass in front of you minute by minute, every day, day after day. Children wearing oversized flip flops, one green, one pink, one torn, one the wrong size.

In the hour that I had been sitting there in quiet peace I heard the soothing swish, swish of sweeping from every direction. Across the street was a tall distinguished black woman with curlers in her hair sweeping uphill from half way down the block, leaving a tidy pile at the corner. I couldn't help but wonder if someone would pick the pile up later or would it simply blow back down the street like homing pigeons flapping back to their roost? The answer came less than a half hour later when the official government street sweeper skimmed it into his broad shovel and dumped it into his bin as he passed by.

Kitty corner from where I was writing there was a woman and man sloshing and sweeping bucket after bucket of water over their front stoop and sidewalk outside their house. Their scrubbed-behind-the-ears pride was evident to all who passed by as they circumnavigated the wet patch that spilled half way into the street.

A young man, clipping along at a deliberate stride stopped quickly, stooped and picked up a plastic cup from the edge of the abandoned lot across the street from me. He examined it carefully, wiped it on his cuff, shrugged his shoulders and put it in his bag. It had been tossed there only moments ago by a different street and stoop slosher. She had deliberately pulled it out of her little pile of swept garbage and tossed it aside, presumably recognizing its true value. This young man was the recipient of her consideration.

Time zips by when you are having fun. It was now just past 8 am and more people were making their way to the street. A man in brilliant white pants carrying 3 buns walked in the house across the street. Two young women in striking brilliant coloured dresses, with matching purses, whispered by with a destination in mind, church?

The government street sweeper returned with a cart and shovel to pick up his previously swept piles.

Desayuno / Breakfast at Roberto's *casa* is presented with the usual generosity of spirit. The fruit, bread, a boiled chickendog each and cheese are wonderful but as usual the hospitality surpasses everything. Roberto, often, at our invitation, sits with us while we eat. The conversations are always interesting and varied, from Cuban economics, to social structure, to explaining the different types of fruit that we have been eating. Oh, and as usual, his coffee is marvelous. He has a fun / funny way of clasping his hands close to his chest and announcing "coffee time". He is a delightfully kind and warm individual.

Music is starting to spill to the street. It is after 9 am now and the long cool shadows are starting to shorten. Heat will soon fill the night-cooled pavement; movement will soon slow to a noonday pause. A bit later I will go halfway down the block and knock at Maria Elena's door and visit with Cristina, her daughter,

José Martí's tomb and monument.

Cemetery with house in background.

José Martí Tomb, Santiago de Cuba.

Changing of the guards at José Martí Tomb, Santiago de Cuba.

and see if she would like to draw on the roof again. Cristina, is a delightful sixteen-year old, shy, pretty, budding artist with ample talent though she has little if any expressionistic training. Her drawing teachers are objectively skill-oriented; straight lines should be straight and representational. I am sure that *"exactimo"* is drummed into her approach to making art. When I introduced her to the idea of placing a fresh sheet of paper on a concrete block as her drawing table she was intriguingly interested. She ran off and returned with sheets of white bond paper and two HB pencils. She was embracing of the resulting, unavoidable textures. Each time we drew together we each sat with our concrete block on our laps and started to draw – rapido, *rapido, no exactimo* – was my only instruction. To my delight she was eager and willing and excited with the project. Her finished drawings were encouraging. With her mother translating for me I offered a challenge – if she produces twenty-five more drawings of the same roof top scene I would buy two of them for 5 pesos each. She would pick which two I would buy, which two she might be most excited by and I would publish them in the CCLA Ambassador or The Envoy.

We drew on the roof top of her home where we all had coffee. Maria Elena, her husband Manuel and their three children and Maria Elena's mother live on the steep slopes of the north side of town. Their roof looks up at the backside of houses and trees, a rich montage of rust, concrete and aging paint. I hope that Cristina will draw with me on the roof later in the afternoon when the sun is cooler and hidden behind the wall of the small room.

Roberto

Roberto is a kind and sensitive man. We talked philosophically about generosity of spirit and human solidarity. He lives these precepts seemingly effortlessly. He has friends that come in and out of his home, apparently at will. While Roberto chats with us, Marie, a spry, slender – maybe wiry, older woman unpacked his market purchases, washed his fruit and put away his goods, she cut a sweet lime into sections and offered them to Eric and me. I had never heard of a sweet lime before. It is not a particularly wonderful fruit but nonetheless eatable unlike trying to eat a fresh face-puckering sour lime. Roberto said Marie is not an employee but a friend. She comes and goes as she likes. One day Roberto and Marie were singing sweet acapella harmonies in the kitchen. He was making dinner and she was tidying the kitchen. The echo of their joy reverberated in the white ceramic tiled kitchen. It was warming to see such brotherly/sisterly camaraderie. It was like listening to the tiny echo of an early black and white movie. Kindness and generosity of spirit spilled from every corner of Roberto's home.

Our four days in Santiago de Cuba should have been four months; it should have been a life time. Like most of Cuba it was as if we were in a science fiction time bubble trapped in the 1950s, warped into the depression of the 20s. Despite the lack, despite the low technology lifestyle it is a magical place of liferhythms that no outsider could possibly understand without first finding a way beyond the buildings and old cars into its heart. Eric and I were lucky to have Roberto and Maria Elena as our guide, leading us past the threshold of poverty into their city, the city of generosity of spirit. In James A. Michener's book "Finding My House in El Cerro" he describes the magic of Havana as "marching backward into the past". Santiago de Cuba imbues that same sense of marching backwards. In many ways time has stood still for this city – lucky for them. I chuckle and search unsuccessfully for a parallel as I think of the Beatles walking backwards across Abbey Road on the eponymous album cover "Abbey Road". The image may have popped into mind while watching a slim young man dressed all in white, wearing an mischievous smile, walking confidently backwards across the street while gazing with Donny-Osmond-puppy-love eyes at a pretty pig-tailed girl in a gold school uniform skirt and crisp white blouse. With no doubt I ponder the notion that they, in their budding desire to move forward, wish they were lavished with what they think of as North American 2010 advantages. Little do they know they are trapped in paradise. With their class mates they are destined to live a proletarian future.

Our stay in Santiago de Cuba was a short one but filled with the calm serenity of low pace meandering, sitting in cafés, dining on the roof of Maria Elena's house and listening to music in the streets. You most likely have heard about the "Bueno Vista Social Club" in Havana and heard the CD or DVD of the same name. Well if you have then you probably have heard about *Casa de la Trova*. One day we were walking downtown – meandering when we heard music overflowing into the street. As we got closer we saw a crowd mulling outside of a club. I am not much of a music connoisseur but this was by far superior to anything I was hearing at resorts or even in public parks. We were drawn into the pulsing crowd. This is where I was stunned by the rhythmic fluidity of Eliades Ochoa and his band.

Another Episode of Generosity

Aside from the wonderful musical experience, that I managed to catch part of on video, I was told later about an episode of generosity that unfolded without me knowing about it until much later. It touched my heart in many ways and reinforced the theme of generosity of spirit that keeps coming up over and over again while in Cuba.

The story starts with our meandering down Calle Heredia at a pace uncharacteristically slow for us in North America. The journey "IS" the destination I keep reminding myself as my mind tries to push me faster than my slowpoke friends who are snailing along through throngs of shoppers towards music spilling to the street. I have to consciously push away the notion that I might miss something if I don't hurry up – what would I miss if I didn't slow down? Just as a joke mantra "Hurry up and slow down" came to mind, a man pushing a handmade buggy passed in front of us. He had two small dogs perched atop his buggy, a wheeled throne the envy of any four-legged prince. Arriving at the musical hubbub we stopped and craned on tiptoes to see past the forty or fifty smiling head-bopping people, stretching to see a classical Cuban music performance. No concert could have exuded more life than this one. No performance could have possibly demanded one's attention more.

After standing in the swaying crowd for a while I crossed the street behind me and sat on the curb beside a 60ish man tapping his toe on the pavement. His face was the colour of burnished mahogany, it shone with delight as he embraced the moment. "*Buenas tardes* – good afternoon", I said as I plunked down beside him leaning on the blue stuccoed building. He held out his hand. Sadly my instinct was to think that he was begging but all he wanted was my hand. Shaking his firm grip and as an echo to his warm smile I said "*Mucho Gusto* – nice to meet you.) *Como estas mi compañero*? - how are you my companion / friend" Smiling back he said "Me? I am good, So you Spanish very very good my friend". With a sense of embarrassment I replied, "*Lo siento señor, mi Español es limitado muy, lo siento.* – I am sorry sir, my Spanish is very limited, I am sorry." "*No hay problema*" he replied. We continued on in English with some polite niceties that concluded with me giving him one peso that he told me he needed to feed his child.

After 15 or 20 minutes I leaned on my new friend and pushed myself to my feet and wandered into the club looking for *mi amigos*. There they were pressed shoulder to shoulder with fellow enthusiasts, Maria Elena's skirt gently swaying to the beat of her hips. This is where I flipped open my camcorder, held it over my head and recorded some footage that has fed me many times since returning.

Well, now then, back to the story of generosity. As it turns out we had all pressed our way into the concert, not realizing that we had to pay. Here we were uninvited guests and we had not reached into our pockets for an entry fee. Unbeknownst to us, Maria Elena's adopted-mother-friend had paid for us without even letting us know. This was kind indeed but when the performer, Eliades Ochoa, heard what his dear friend had done he reached into his pocket and pressed our entry fee into her hand. Here we were now the guest of the main performer, a man of international renown, and we didn't even know it. All of this was revealed to us later by Maria Elena. Pretty cool being paid for by one of the icons of Cuban classical music. Eric went to his house the next day in search of his autograph on a cd that he bought at *Casa de la Trova* but to his disappointment he was not in.

Cuba and the Bent Wheel Parallel

Most parallels and metaphors are fraught with pitfalls that can only partly represent or express what one is trying to say. Despite this, I will try to draw a simple contrast between my bent wheel story and Cuba as a nation. During this trip, the back wheel of my bike was bent out of ride able shape because of, what I was quick to label as, poor handling of my bike by the bus company that transported Eric and me back to Holguín from Santiago. It was my human nature to quickly label myself as a victim of the employee that loaded my bike, further I was a victim of the bus company that employed and trained the individual and then of course that meant I was a victim of Cuba because everyone is ultimately an employee of the state. In the end, it took me a day or two to pull myself from under being a victim of anything other than my lack of foresight. If I had simply removed both wheels instead of just the front wheel, the back wheel would have, most certainly, not been bent. I have spent much of my life trying to learn to take responsibility for outcomes and not be a victim. This was a valuable experience for me.

Through this happenstance, I started to ask myself a few fundamental questions. What is the connection between victim and ego? Why are our egos so connected to our success or failure or even a bent wheel? Are we afraid of judgment by others or afraid of our own rigid self-condemnation for wrong choices? Does every person, including country leaders have their rationale for their country's successes and failures? I am thinking of the Fidel Castro régime, the decades long USA embargo, and the roles of victim and victimizer.

It seems to me as I have travelled around Cuba for the last decade and a half that part of Fidel Castro's success has come from the USA embargo. Without the embargo, he might not have had the opportunity to be a victim and disguise his failings as a leader. First, he was the victim of the Batista régime. He, apparently, justifiably, used ruthless force to overthrow the obvious injustices though pacifists like Gandhi or Martin Luther King, might have used peaceful means. In the process of overthrowing the government, he agitated many rich

Cubans that fled to the USA where their gathered powers influenced their new USA government – the embargo was born.

I do not have any answers, just growing questions. Was there a different political / social model other than the Soviet communist model and returning all of the land and wealth to the country / to the people? Is there a socialist model with capitalist leanings that could have worked better? Is there a single communist / socialist country that has survived and thrived? Was it simply leadership failings that caused other communist countries to fail or is the communist model itself flawed?

Yes, more and more questions and never a simple answer in sight. I admire much of what the Fidel Castro régime has accomplished including his education system. I admire the theory behind the medical system even though plagued with lack of supplies and limited resources that has led to, sometimes, squalor hospital conditions. Let me go back to one of the first questions. Does every person, including country leaders have their rationale for their successes and failures? Fidel Castro pounded his people with the notion that Cuba was in shambles economically because of one primary force – the USA embargo.

Fidel might best thank heaven for the USA embargo for providing him with the opportunity to be a victim. Without this victimization opportunity, he would have to look at himself square in the mirror and wonder what he was doing wrong with his leadership in following the communist model so rigidly or, hey, maybe the question

Roberto

Maria Elena

A stranger on the streets of Santiago de Cuba.

Eliades Ochoa

truly should be, is the Cuban economic shambles strictly because of the USA embargo? Is it possible that Cuba's economic stability would be greatly improved without the USA embargo? We will never know.

Remember what I said in the preface – "I can't always promise to tell it as it is but I can always promise to tell how I see it." I see roofs blown off houses that have never been repaired – low tech and no money would solve that. I see disgusting toilets in universities and other public buildings – a pail of water and a brush would solve that. Sorry Fidel but you preached value in being a victim. Now you have a generation of not-so-devoted citizens that feel they are a victim of you and now my bike wheel is a victim of you. Your employee insisted that I pay a bicycle loading fee. I told him that my bicycle was included in the fee I just paid. In the end I realized that the extra fee was going straight into his pocket. I would have gladly paid an official extra fee for carrying my bike if it had included some sort of rack and actual real care had been given to the protection of my bike but he did not care. Was the failing communist model of government responsible for my bent wheel?

A Trip to Gibara

Gibara is pronounced "He-Bar-ah" is a marvelous ghost town of a coastal city, neither thriving nor dead. One might say it lies in a coma. It is the ghost that hovers in the mist as a hurricane-traumatized city that once was. It boasts of being the first place where Christopher

Columbus stopped when he discovered the Americas, but then again, so do a few other Cuban cities.

Gibara is important enough as one of my favorite Cuban haunts that I wanted to take Eric to visit my friend Jorge and show him this unpolished gem with a bit of a loose setting. Eric grew up on the east coast of Canada. I thought he would appreciate this rugged link to the sea that is such a serenely pleasant part of Cuba. As a "once-was" city you can see the past in the modestly grand cathedral in the main square, the humble museum and its hanging-on-by-a-thread-crumbling architecture that echoes a better, more prosperous past. Now after years of silent slumber Gibara is going through a gentle awakening, a calm resurgence from its near-death experience.

With a bit of brotherly arm twisting Eric and I managed to convince our dear Cuban friend, Miriam, to join us for the overnight trip. Miriam is not old enough to be a mother figure but maybe rather an aunt. She might be better described as a dear friend of the family.

She is a chatty well dressed colour coordinated, fun but proper woman. The day of our departure, Eric and I drove to Miriam's house in a cab. I stood at the bottom of her second story stairs and called up to her in my best melodramatic British gay drawl I could muster – "Miirrriaaam, Miriam darling are you ready for a splendid time in Gibara with Eric and me, Miirrriaaam, darling." As I discovered later, poor Miriam was devastated by the tongue-wagging gossip that erupted in her neighbourhood on her departure with two foreign men.

Because of Cuban laws she would stay at my friend Jorge's *casa particular* registered only for Cubans and we would have to stay at a *casa* registered for tourists arranged for us by Jorge. Every time I am confronted by this inequality I seethe with condemnation of the Castro dictatorship but quietly bite my tongue in resignation. In a previous Cuban memoir entitled "From Cross Hill" I include a blatant metaphoric allegory about green cows and blue cows and how they shall never mix except on the most superficial of levels. As much as I love Cuba, its people and even what Castro has done for his people I fume over what I perceive as unfair, shallow, fear-ridden, treatment of its people but then again I am only an outsider, a visitor bringing my biased personal sensibilities to the country. Maybe I will never know enough about running a country to know the value of segregationism.

A Visit to the Caves of Gibara

Eric, Miriam, Jorge and I, guided by Jesus Luz (the name Jesus in Spanish sounds like "Hose-ae" and Luz translates as Light), descended into the bowels of Gibara – yeah I know that is a bit of a dramatic cliché but it at least, hopefully, sparks your interest in our spelunking expedition. Oh and yes the metaphoric parallel of being led by "Jesus of Light" does not escape me. First we wove our way up through city streets to the near-top of the city. Before reaching the top we exited the tranquil thoroughfares into a country path. After passing through a cleverly-quaint hand-built turnstile we zigzagged through tall grass, past thorny cactii, over stumbling rocks and stumps until we finally arrived at an immense black yawning hole in the ground surrounded by lush vegetation. This hole was not at all inviting. We five stood around it looking deep to the red trampled floors of the first upper vault. A few more paces down the overgrown path took us to a step-down entrance that even a child could navigate. We found ourselves in the bungalow size vault with a huge hole in the ceiling through which we had just gazed. After wandering around in awe, examining barren red walls stripped clear of crystals, we donned our head-gear lights and slowly, cautiously, headed into dark.

    I felt like a privileged child. A young lad on an adventure that none of my friends would believe when I returned to school. I was Tom Sawyer with Huck Finn hiding out from the murderous Injun Joe. Here I was fifty-five living life to my fullest – Thrilled! The only thing that separated us from the abyss of death was a fist full of AA batteries and controlling our fear. From the first large vault we ducked and stooped our way down, down narrow low passages to another large, small-house size, echoing theatre. The air was getting heavier and hotter as we descended. Sweat was beading, dripping from my brow off the end of my nose as we stooped lower, further, into the black of our imagination. We had been in the lifeless depths for only twenty minutes. Time stood still as we groped our way deeper into the earth in bowed reverence watching the incandescent blur at our feet grow imperceptibly dimmer. We glanced up from moment to moment to avoid the too-close ceiling that made us stoop. I am six-foot-three inches tall and soon had a few bruises from dripping outcrops. Lumpy ravaged hallways, stripped of crystals, gouged from mother earth's womb led us deeper, deeper, hotter. Another twenty minutes later, deeper, we were at the end of our journey in a third echoing vault. When we finally stood upright and listened past our own breath, past our own heartbeats we could hear a distant drip, drip echoing from the distant black. Our beams of light revealed pools of water down, further down past a treacherous knee-scraping descent. Fingers dipped, dabbed to tongue, reveal it is the ocean. We have trudged, descended hundreds of feet down, hundreds of feet under the city all the way to the sea. Somewhere through these submerged inky depths, never to be explored passages, is an underwater path out to the open sea.

The Silence of Black

Though dark and deep, this Gibara spelunking experience was very different from the one that we had on a CCLA trip a couple of years ago. It was our second CCLA trip to Havana in 2008 when we took a day trip to the Bellamar Caves of Matanzas. Google that phrase and you will find that the caves are incredible but none the less a tourist trap. We arrived by bus with my little Cuban brother Wency guiding us – thank you Wency. We lined up with seventy-five to a hundred tourists and Cuban nationals. We then waited in line to get into the building and then again to pass down a set of stairs into an incandescent glowing cave. The sight was stupendous and well worth the few pesos and the wait. The caves were humungous and filled with glistening crystals but the din of chatter by onlookers was painfully disappointing. A tour guide spoke in Spanish talking about the thousands upon hundreds of thousands of years that Mother Nature took to manufacture the cathedral.

It did not take me very long to get bored with the extravaganza and find myself wandering into unlit caves as far away from the hubbub and racket as possible. Finally after a few minutes of deep quiet I realized that it had gotten rather dark and I could no longer see my feet. I am not a man who is afraid of a little adventure so the question was not unreasonable for me to ask – Do I push forward further into the quiet damp or do I turn around and return to the prattle of the swarming masses? I have never been one for following rules, direction, order, so why start now? Within a few steps there was not a speck of light, neither forward or back, up or down. It was pitch black – absolutely incredible. I was in the pit of the planet standing in infinity and all I could see was nothing – absolutely notttthhhhing. Close your eyes or open them. Put hands over your eyes. It was all the same. Do you remember laying in bed as a child passing your hand in front of your face wondering if you could actually see an outline or not? Was it your imagination that you saw an aura shimmer in the dark? In this dark there was no aura. There was no mental trickery that could make me think that there was a speck of light and I was all alone. Not a sound other than my own breath filled the cave or was it even a cave. I was all alone in the silence and the dark. It was magnificent. I have never felt such joyous peace as listening and looking and having nothing come back. In the silence of this cave black became beautiful. We were taught in school that black was the absence of colour and colour required light. I was now feeling, feeling for the first time that this black was not just the absence of light but was also the absence of sound. What an experiential thrill!

So now I have spun around in different directions looking and seeing nothing and now I have no idea of which direction I came or want to go even if I wanted to grope my way back along the crystal corridor. All I wanted to do was lay down on the cool damp floor of my cave, relax in the silent *negro* and maybe fall into a peaceful sleep, but don't forget that I am an adult – at least part of me is. I knew that if I stayed much longer letting my id dissolve into this experiential black hole of nothing that people would start wondering where I was. Had I fallen over one of the guard rails into a ten-thousand foot drop into molten lava and was evaporated into ions? I chuckle and swing my camera in front of me and flash. I recognize the turn in the path from where I had just come so the child ego goes in the opposite direction. I flash again and take a few more stooping steps, guarding my head and face with every step. Another flash, another few steps, another flash. This was kind of fun, another flash, another flash.

Hmm I wonder just how many flashes this battery has left. Mental calculations start lighting up in my mind. My battery was this full, I had already taken this many flashes, the manual said, if I remember correctly, that I had plenty of flashes left before I was stranded and had to wait for rescue. I smile and chuckle again – that would be humiliating. One flash and six steps or should I just keep going until I bump into something? Another flash, another flash. Then there was the flash that did not totally turn off. Was that my arm in front of me? Is that a speck of light at the end of the proverbial tunnel? It was almost disappointing when I could walk free with head up at a normal stride.

The thrill of experiencing the silence of *negro*, black was far more thrilling than any sense of being lost or finding my way back into light. While I was grateful to be back in the light looking for my lost friends, I was more grateful for the utter absence of fear. It was simply a thrill that I am glad I had. To use my wife's word, it was maybe actually "fun" though for me thrill and fun are not quite synonymous. By the end of the day and a few more pictures I discovered my camera battery was dead. I smiled and chuckled again quietly to myself.

Roof top drawing by Cristina.

Roof top drawing by Tai.

Maria Elena, Eric and me on our departure day.

Maria Elena

Portrait of a Gibara girl.

Santiago de Cuba

Eric browsing.

Richard M. Grove

2008 – Cuevas de Bellamar
The Caves of Bellemar

Alone in silent awe
swallowed by dank depths
of vaulted stillness.
Unseen drips percolate
plat,   plat,   plat

Middle-age exhilaration stirs.
Primeval stillness swells
my teenage imagination
plat,   plat,   plat

Ducking conformity I escape
the clatter, the throng
of tourist enthusiasm
plat,   plat,   plat

Out of sight from all
I disappear into silent gulf
of endless black
plat,   plat,   plat

The voice of petrified skeletons
refugees of 15th century Spanish tyranny
echo in crystalline prehistoric mystery
plat,   plat,   plat

Trapped in Paradise: Views of My Cuba

Relishing my blind shuffle
I wonder just for a moment
if this is my midnight
plat,   plat,   plat

Cradled by blind trust
of electronic camera flash
I take six small caution steps
flash again, six more
plat,   plat,   plat

I creep in stooped marvel.
There is no fear spurred
by self-imposed solitude
plat,   plat,   plat

My groping foray into
the unknown lasted
a 20-minute lifetime
plat,   plat,   plat

Some friends regaled
my adventure as brave
others suggested stupid
I remain undaunted
by this thrill of my own making

Miriam

Jorge

Jorge, Miriam and Eric.

Jorge, Miriam, Jesus and Eric after spelunking.

Entrance to the caves, Jorge and Eric.

Laundry and the Dead Windmill

From Miriam's *casa*, Jorge's house, the three of us Gibara visitors slowly meandered west along the coast in search of visual adventures. The first thing that we were struck by was the hurricane-damaged, war-torn houses and street. Sections of the road and sidewalk had been ripped out by devastating waves. In some cases only the shell of houses stood with the inhabitants still living within crumbling walls – open to the sun and moon. Clean laundry, bright colours and sparkling whites were strung from house to house, from post to shed. It was obvious that pride has survived the many beatings the community has received over the decades.

Further along we arrive at an Olympic-size swimming pool with a hurricane-tossed-car-size boulder in the middle of the now empty cracked former glory. Further along still is the rusted shattered hulk of an ocean liner that has been tossed like a toy onto the rocky shore. Over time it moves up or down the shore, in or out, at the wind and wave's command. Even further along are the motionless arms of a gentle giant, a huge windmill frozen in time stretching, disobedient to the wind's demands. I have seen this rusting relic of modern technology poised for years. Wind rushing through its outstretched blades in vain.

Everywhere we turned there was devastation that might never be repaired but beyond this facade of rack and ruin are smiling faces of survivors. Generations of hope greeted us with outstretched generosity. If all they could offer was a smile and a hello then that is what they freely gave. Never was there an outstretched hand of desperation begging with hope.

A Trip to a Distant Farm

Today, Dec 22nd, my last Tuesday before leaving for Canada, a friend hired a car for a day trip to visit his father's farm. Except for the loving company that filled the car the trip was primitive, lacking in grace and dignity from the moment we set out to the moment that I arrived back to *mi casa*. Let me start with the potholes. I have been on Cuban potholed roads before, in fact these very roads five years ago. I understand potholes and I understand an economic drought that will prevent the fixing of potholes but in my opinion, I think they should just not even try to fill these potholes anymore. Ten years of not fixing potholes has left potholes in the moral fiber of the people that have to travel this road. There is a pavement chewing machine that can easily turn pavement into gravel. This machine can break up the pavement and return this ungraceful, undignified road back to a gravel road for less money than they are spending on pothole repairs. A gravel road can have grace and dignity and on top of that it is easier and cheaper to maintain. Even a potholed gravel road can have grace but potholes, beside potholes, inside of potholes, surrounded by potholes, on an ancient emaciated road driving out of the past has no grace and no dignity. It spells despair, and despair is graceless. I am quite willing to feel sad that Cuba built a highway, with Russian rupees, and that they had no crystal ball to see that the Russian economic support would dry up but is it not time to fully recognize this and return to a former glory of having a fine gravel road?

Let's get beyond potholes and let's just arrive at the farm. We drove in through a graceless rusty iron gate. Iron gates can be rusty and still have grace and dignity but when an iron gate is flopping, hingeless from disregard then there is no grace. It spells despair.

When I said the day had no grace and dignity I was hasty in my pronouncement. There was grace and dignity in the land. The field that we traversed after turning off of the muddy road swelled with grace and dignity. It was hanging with grey when we arrived, raining only slightly but the majesty of the land could still be seen through the veil. Some of us got out of the thirty-five year old Lada as soon as we slowed over the swaying grass field. We stepped from aging steel on to the land. We wanted to walk in the magnificence. Following behind the blue Lada, we headed to the house. We strode through damp grass that glowed with clinging mist. We gazed past a cactus fence row to the splendor of Royal Palms swaying with notable dignity in the distance. Even the pond lined with mud from trudging drinking animals sparkled with grace as fingers of rain dotted the surface like water-striders walking on water. Yellow flowering shrubs scattered along the perimeter whispered with poetry. Even the two small houses commonly called bohíos, a native Indian word for thatched roof house, in the distance had a simple sense of beauty. All of this was grace, poetry in motion.

We were living the poetry as we moved and then the poetry stopped. It utterly stopped as we walked through the low-slung gate made of silver-aging sticks. Those sticks had grace. The line that the gate drew in the hard red earth had a gentle grace but the line said all grace will stop from here forward. It said henceforth all that is touched by people will be graceless, unpoetic, grim. All will be the expression of despair, desolation and despondency. All will be gloom.

It was not because of the drizzling rain and the grey that hung low in the air like wet hair trying to drag our spirits down. It was the dim uninviting, uninspiring, lifeless surroundings of the house lit by a single waning light bulb dangling over the table. I had once before, five years previously, been to this house and there was a different sense of life. Now everything and everywhere was grimy with disregard. It was as if contempt and disdain ruled the house. I could not wait to leave. After a few minutes we went out to the "*rancho*", as my friend called it. The rancho was separate from the house, an open-air roofed area. Two oxen ploughs were stored there, some firewood, some broken down implements, a wobbling workbench, long sticks were stored in the rafters. All of this on its own does not sound all that different from some sheds at the back of a house or beside the barn but the fact is it was graceless. Nothing seemed to have a proper place. Day's earlier in Gibara, we were in Jorge's tiny fishing-tack shack. A small room attached to the back of the house. It was filled with grace. Everything was in a proper place. It did not matter that the boards for the shelf were old, that the nail hook was rusty. The important thing is that everything had a purpose and a place. In the rancho things were tossed with disregard rather than stored. The coffee type grinder, bolted to the wobbling bench was broken or at least falling apart with pieces lying on the dirt floor. I started to think of the potholes again. Broken this or that were stacked on top of other broken this or that. One can tell the difference between piles of disorder and piles of work in progress. That's the think, there was no progress. Progress is grace in action. The house had not been cleaned and put in order and neither had the *rancho*.

Cultural Differences

There are many cultural differences between Canada and Cuba. One that keeps popping up at dinner times is the feeding of guests first, in fact the culture of feeding people in a hierarchical order is common when you are invited out to a home. This cultural difference showed up at both lunch and dinner that day at the farm. The feeding order is often, seat and feed the guests first, while the hostess and often the host take care of kitchen matters. "Eat, have more, there is plenty." was uttered many times by the father at the head of the table. Often the man of the house is served with the guests while he directs the wife to get the guests more. This was certainly the case at the farm. "The wife" eventually sat off to the side with her plate on her lap after we were almost finished. It was suggested to me later that there might have been a shortage of plates or chairs but she was sitting and eating at the same time as us and it was not from a pot.

The son who killed and very skillfully butchered the pig, skewered the pig on the post for roasting, prepared the fire, minded the fire during the long roasting process and even chopped the firewood for the fire was allocated to carving the roasted pig and then eating with his wife only after we had eaten and the table was cleared. Was this the case because there were insufficient plates and chairs? Not likely. As he lived only yards away he could have easily brought over a plate and chair for both his wife and himself. I remember being invited to a big family party where I was also invited to bring a plate and a chair as were other guests. The hierarchical order for this family clearly placed him at the bottom rung of the ladder. A different culture would have honoured this man and insisted he have a place at the head of the table.

My feeling was that someone needed to tip the ladder on its side to equalize everyone. Further to the hierarchical equation, his wife scooped up some scraps of meat and fat into a plastic bag that was set aside to go to their house. The entire meal lacked any sense of grace or dignity. I felt awkward and out of sorts the entire meal. My hierarchical placement was high on the ladder simply because I was the foreigner visitor. As I was eating I was thinking that the dogs were also on the hierarchical ladder but at least they don't have the social understanding other than sensing their lowest rung standing. Scraps were tossed out the door to the threshold waiting dogs. Their hierarchical order was dictated by brute strength and sharp teeth.

The graceless meal was finally finished and it was time to go home. The day-long drizzle still hung like wet muslin. The man that drove the hired car thought it prudent to stay parked about two miles down the now impossibly muddy rutted road; perched at the end of the gravel section. This strategy ensured we would get home that night. Thank heavens for his wisdom. The steel grey day hovered with heavy clouds the colour of wet concrete.

To transport us from the farm house to the car an ancient, creaky oxen drawn cart was hired to drag us through the now drizzling ebony night, through calf deep mud. As fun and adventurous as this might have been the word grace and dignity could never, in a million years, have been used to describe the half hour escapade of escape. To add some levity to the irony of being dragged through the mud two days before Christmas I started singing Christmas carols, starting with "Rudolf the Red Nosed Reindeer" followed by "I Am Dreaming of a White Christmas" and "The Little Drummer Boy" for which no one knew the words including myself. I hope that this added a bit of humour and maybe even a bit of grace to the otherwise slippery, slimy, mucky, hang-on-for-dear-life experience. Tossed and ruffled we travelled from the 1400s back to the parked car and headed back to the city. I guess it is hardly necessary for me to say that we dodged potholes the rest of the way home, slowing to a crawl from time to time so we could drive in to a pothole and out the other side.

Viva la Revolución

After all of these years the Revolution is still omnipresent in Cuba. "Viva la Revolución" means "Long live the Revolution". It is an ever-present part of Cuban culture. This ubiquitous slogan still shows up in banners and murals, parades, speeches and rallies, pop art and serious art, as well as music of every genre. This Cuban cultural tide has turned, over the past 50 years, into a sociological phenomenon that has united its people of all ages, of every job description and level of education. The people of Cuba are still fueled by this culture of survival that the revolution fosters at every turn and it isn't going to stop anytime soon. Fidel Castro said, sometime in the 60s, that he will shave off his beard when the revolution is finally won; he still proudly wears his beard with distinction and will most certainly be buried with an untanned chin.

In all of my travels through Cuba, and certainly on this past bike trip, there are faded and paint-peeled murals professing the importance and endurance of the revolution. In a couple of cases over the years I have seen a mural say "*Vivo la Revolución*" (vivo, with an "o") which would translate as "I live the Revolution". These time-battered murals may be a stark symbol of revolutionary starvation but it should be noted that they have not been scraped off or painted over, nor have they been graffitied. They are the dimming reminder that the revolution is still alive even if starving. Murals of every size and level of sophistication cover a myriad of paintable surfaces from high-rise city banners to dilapidated country bus shelters. Some new revolutionary billboards that profess the resilience of the Cuban people point past the proud hurricane battered Malicon of Havana, past the thrashing sea, to the USA. It is like a middle finger waving over the heads of Cuban traffic to the unseen enemy.

A starving revolution is better than no revolution at all. What is the value of a revolution if not to draw the people into the fold of loving their leader and their country? A revolution no matter how impoverished will at least serve to fortify the people and give purpose to their poverty. A proud resilient people will always march to a revolutionary rally rather than to a rebellious revolt. A proud people with a united cause, a despised enemy, will link arms and wave the flag of hope together but more importantly, will stay loyal to their united cause of survival.

There was no Squeal of a Pig

I got up just before 6 am to start my packing for my afternoon departure back to chilly Canada. In some ways it was a sad day. I had to disassemble and pack my bicycle, *mi bicicleta*, into the tattered box that I arrived with; I had to pack my suitcase and organize the presents that I had brought for friends. Breakfast was the normal wonderful lush fruit, orange juice, dark-roasted Cuban coffee and buns that I had grown to expect every morning. I think that I might take some peanut butter with me the next trip. I ate less than I might normally as I was expected at Manuel's for a 10 am turkey brunch.

Such wonderful friends I have remembering my comment that turkey is a North American Christmas tradition – they brought a turkey fresh from Manuel's father's farm and boiled it into a delicious soup. It was not exactly the golden-roasted-turkey-dinner tradition but the love that it was cooked with made up for the fact that they did not have a roasting pan, let alone an oven to put it in. It was my absolute delight to be in Cuba on Christmas morning with my dearest of friends. I could hardly wish for anything more special.

The first thing that I noticed after the rooster's crow greeted me was the utter absence of other noises. It was so very quiet. There was a distinct absence of traffic noises being Christmas morning but the quiet was more than that. The neighbourhood dogs, for the most part, had not started to yelp and children were still in bed. All of this peace was to be expected on Christmas morning but still there was a penetrating quiet, an uncanny stillness that I could not quite put my finger on until *mi casa* particular host offered me some ham for breakfast – then it dawned on me. There was no squeal of a pig anywhere to be heard. Neither the pig next door, the pig three or four yards over or the pig a block away gave a snort or squeal. This was very unusual indeed. Usually the morning was filled with the feeding-frenzy squeals of delight from neighbourhood pigs in every direction. I am sure that the conspicuous absence of pig noises was not to do with a Cuban tradition of pigs sleeping in on the blessed Christmas morn. As I discovered later the quietude definitely had something to do with Christmas traditions and nothing to do with a pig's dreamy languor. It had all to do with pigs being invited as the guest of honour or, should I say, as the main course the night before. In Cuba they start six months earlier by raising a baby pig for the explicit purpose of roasting it on a pole on Christmas Eve.

Brunch included our dear friend Miriam and even Eric in his absence through his stories and hilarities. We found ourselves in belly-laughing stitches making up even more lines for Eric's fictitious book that he won't write – "Most Common English/Spanish Translated

Phrases". Eric even used some of these while meeting strangers in Santiago de Cuba – "Hello, my sister weighs 2000 pounds", was his favorite. We spent the better part of an hour busting our gut making up new lines for his book. "Would you please take the onions out of my pants," "Could you please put peas up your nose before speaking to me."

Superman pajamas with requisite cape, dinosaurs, an unfriendly plastic snake, a truck and cars, pencils, markers and more were followed by the stomping disappointment that Santa could not carry more in his blue, twenty-five year old flying Russian Lada. As generous as Santa is he can never, ever meet the expectations of a single child. The end of a wonderfully memorable Christmas morning was met with tears, mine, as I road off with Antonio in his pre-arranged cab. We picked up my boxed bicycle and suitcases at *mi casa* and headed to the airport.

The usual airport lineups and four-hour flight gave me plenty of time to ponder the end of another wonderful month-long trip with my precious Cuban family. Despite its political and economic flaws I had fallen deeper in love with Cuba than ever before. Even though I would be returning in only a matter of weeks with the group of Canada Cuba Literary Alliance Members I was sad, sad for many reasons. Sad because time and ocean makes it impossible to for me to come and go as often as I like. Sad because my economic standing does not allow me the freedom to pop in to see my Cuban friends at will. Even though these childlike melancholies are easily swept from the adult mind there is a bigger, much more ponderable sadness worth considering. That is the sadness that so many of my Cuban friends are stuck on this wonderful island for the rest of their lives with no recourse other than to live out their lives the way "The Revolution" has dictated. I was brought to welling eyes contemplating the fact that my dear friends would be forever trapped in paradise.

Soon to be dinner.

Note:
CUC – Cuban Convertible Pesos = $1USA
Cuban Peso / People's Peso = 25 pesos to 1 CUC
The CUC is often called the "Cook"

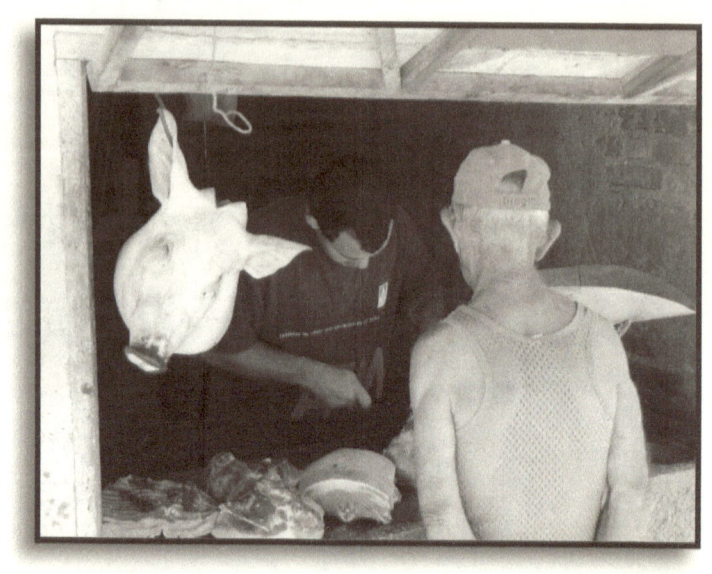

Saddle Mountain seen from Gibara Bay.

Pablo, Manuel and Adonay.

Manuel's father and step mother with Adaonay, and Sister-in-law in back left.

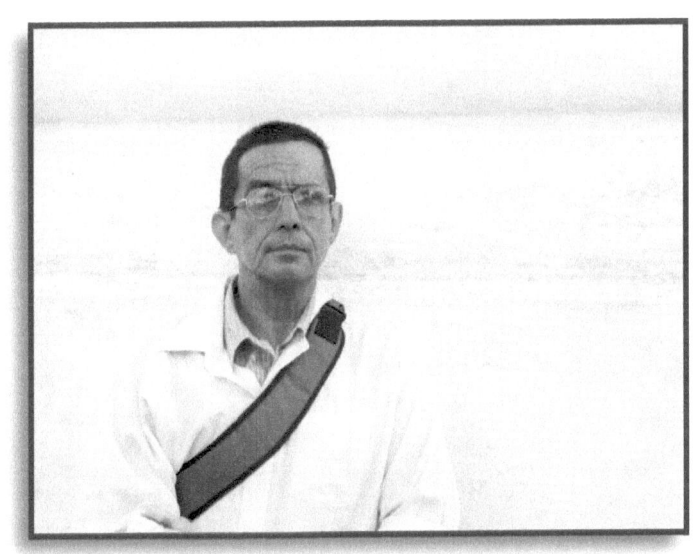

Manuel

Ernesto, Manue's half brother.

Manuel's son Pablo, my Godson.

Manuel with sons, Alejandro and Pablo.

Victor, Manuel's son.

Miriam, Adonay and Maria Elana.

Afterword

The image above, of the split rock with the tree growing out of it, is a photo I took at a sculpture garden while on a CCLA trip to Santiago de Cuba. While skimming through my thousands of photographs of Cuba looking for the perfect image for the cover of this book, this one jumped out at me. My roots as an artist are in pottery and sculpture. I was attracted to the rugged weight of the rock and the tree; I was attracted to its volume, its texture and colour. I took a quick snapshot as I dashed back to the murmuring tour bus that was idly, waiting for the last few of us stragglers. We would soon be returned to the air conditioned comfort of our all-inclusive resort for a plate-heaping dinner. In the end, for a variety of reasons, I decided to include this image on the inside of the book rather than on the cover but it still stands strong for me as a metaphor.

The metaphor springing from this image is perfect on many levels. The rock, being Cuba, is cracked but still solid. It is time-stained but none the less beautiful and perfect – in fact the patina of time makes the rock / Cuba even more beautiful. On the other hand the rock might also be the heavy weight of the USA. Despite the crippling load, Cuba still manages to push forth and survive, in fact more than survive by continuing to grow in an unpredicted and even astonishing way. The tree is also the Cuban people, still growing, still surviving, still making their way despite the burden that the country, the rock, places on them. The tree cannot be prevented from being the perfect manifestation of endurance, perseverance and determination. Nothing can hold the Cuban people down; no country, no foreign political arm, no hurricane, drought or political ideology. They grow and survive beautifully against all odds. And what of the little plants that are surviving, creeping from under the rock? What of the parched grass field where the rock rests or the nubbled navel in the tree where a branch once grew? What of the dark shadow that is in the depths of the rock's cleave or the beating sun that day after day warms and sooths her?

Despite these layers and layers of metaphors, sometimes a tree is just a tree, sometimes a rock a rock. Even on this objective level they are both beautiful. Simply being what they are in the most straightforward, uncomplicated way it is simply a Cuban tree growing from a Cuban rock in the Cuban landscape; a snapshot by a Canadian tourist trying to understand the complexities of centuries. It was my pleasure to see the rock and the tree on its many metaphoric levels as well as simply as a tree and a rock on a sunny day in Cuba.

Biographical Sketch of Author

Richard M. Grove / Tai
photo by Kim Grove

Richard M. Grove, otherwise known to friends as Tai, was born into an artist family in Hamilton, Ontario, on October 7, 1953. With both parents artists and gallery owners he had a unique and early introduction into the world of visual art. His first experience with art was with photography when at the age of thirteen he purchased, with his father's enthusiasm and help, his first single lens reflex camera. Over the ensuing years, after leaving high school, he studied pottery at Mohawk College, design and pottery at Sheridan College, leading to his graduation in 1984 from the Experimental Arts Department at Ontario College of Art. In 1994 he graduated with honours from the Humber College, Arts Administration diploma program. In 2002 he returned to school to study computer courses relating to publishing.

Since graduating from OCA, Richard has exhibited in more than twenty solo and group exhibitions in Hamilton, Toronto, Boston, Calgary and Grand Prairie. He has his art in over thirty corporate collections across Canada, the most prominent of which are Esso Resources, Continental Insurance, Alberta Energy Corporation and Calgary District Hospital Group. These four companies alone represent a collection of almost thirty pieces of his work. Among the many corporate collections are six commissions of different styles and mediums ranging from pastel on paper to acrylic on canvas.

His photography and digital paintings have been featured on the cover of almost 50 books and periodicals. His book of digital paintings and poetry entitled "Sky Over Presqu'ile" was published in 2003, "Substantiality" a book of digital paintings was published in 2006 with a book of photography entitled "Oxido Rojo" released in the fall of 2006 followed by a book of Photography entitled "terra firma" in the same year.

Along with his visual art, Richard has been writing poetry seriously for decades and has had over 100 of his poems published in periodicals and in over 30 anthologies from around the world. Including his poetry and photography he has 10 titles to his name. To mention only two of his poetry titles, his book entitled "Beyond Fear and Anger" was released in 1997 and his book "Poems For Jack" was released in 2002. He is also the author of numerous books with metaphysical themes including "The Mind–Body Connection", "Metaphysical Healing For a Secular Age" and "A Spiritual Study of Body".

He is an editor and publisher and runs a growing publishing company, Hidden Brook Press, from which he publishes books of every genre for authors around the world. Aside from being a published poet, Richard has also exhibited his poetry in acrylic on paper paintings as well as in audio sculptures. For his poetry and prose, Richard has won a few small prizes and honourable mentions as well as a finalist spot in contest anthologies. For his short stories he has won a top ten prize.

Richard is the founder of the Canadian Poet Registry, an archival information website that lists Canadian poets including: biographical information, their book titles and awards. One can view this website at -www.hiddenbrookpress.com/Registry.htm. He was an active member of the Canadian Poetry Association (CPA) for ten years serving on the executive for seven years including five as President. He is the founding president of both the CCLA (2004) – Canada Cuba Literary Alliance – www.CanadaCubaLiteraryAlliance.org and the Brighton Arts Council (BAC). The CCLA has an international membership and boasts a full-colour literary journal called The Ambassador and a literary e-newsletter called The Envoy.

Richard has also been a public speaker MCing poetry readings and other literary events. He has been invited by a number of literary groups as Feature Speaker on various topics in Cuba, Germany, USA, New Zealand and Canada. He was also the Feature Author in the October 1998 issue of "The Treasure Chest" published out of Virginia, USA and Feature Poet in "Poetry Canada" in 2004.

Richard lives with his wife, also a writer / editor, Kim, in Presqu'ile Provincial Park situated halfway between Toronto and Kingston, south of the 401 hwy where they run a B&B for authors, artists and birders. Their location is a constant inspiration for their work. You can find them at – www.hiddenbrookpress.com/Cottage-hbpRetreat.html.

Tai's Movies on YouTube (*find more soon*)

— End of Winter in Presqu'ile –
http://www.youtube.com/watch?v=pxcj5G0evZQ
— José Martí Changing of the guards
http://www.youtube.com/watch?v=EC2FOKKM1Fw
— José Martí Monument 2011
http://www.youtube.com/watch?v=M2oKXw-O5KE

Books by Richard M. Grove

- Beyond Fear and Anger
- Poems For Jack: Poems for the Poetically Challenged
- A View of Contrasts: Cuba Poems
- The Mind Body Connection
- Sky Over Presqu'ile
- terra firma
- Oxido Rojo
- Substantiality
- A Spiritual Study of Body
- The Family Reunion
- From Cross Hill
- Psycho Babble and the Consternations of Life
- a trip to banes, Cuba, 2002
- Trapped In Paradise – Views of My Cuba

Richard M. Grove / Tai
photo by Christopher Grove

www.ingramcontent.com/pod-product-compliance
Lightning Source LLC
Chambersburg PA
CBHW021110080526
44587CB00010B/468